A Question of Care

THE CHANGING FACE OF THE NATIONAL HEALTH SERVICE

Nick Davidson

MICHAEL JOSEPH
London

First published in Great Britain by Michael Joseph Ltd
27 Wrights Lane, London W8
1987

British Library Cataloguing in Publication Data

Davidson, Nick
    A question of care: the changing face of
    the National Health Service
    1. National Health Service (Great Britain)
    I. Title
    362.1'0941   RA395.G6
    ISBN 0-7181-2586-X

Typeset by Cambrian Typesettrs, Frimley, Surrey
Printed in Great Britain by Richard Clay Ltd, Bungay, Suffolk

Contents

Acknowledgements

This book would not have been possible without the co-operation of Haringey Health Authority and its staff. I would like to thank Lawrence Bains, district chairman, Barbara Young, former district administrator and her successor, Katherine McGlaughlin, for allowing me to poke around. They almost certainly do not agree with some of what I have said, or the conclusions I have drawn, but they were nevertheless generous with their time and put no restrictions in my way. Many other people from the health district have also been helpful. In particular, I learned a great deal from Dr Sandy Pringle, Peter Tinsley, Colin Kerr, Dr George Marsh, Dr Anthony Griew, Dot Spence, Clive Amos and Mike Quinn. Navarro Colaco, administrator of the Enfield and Haringey family practitioner committee, gave me much help and time, as did Lilias Gillies of Haringey community health council, Malcolm Scott, nursing officer at Claybury Hospital, Leslie Fisher and Daisey Eyres of the local NUPE branch, David Townsend, director of social services for Haringey and Haringey social service's home help organisers for the Tottenham area. Stephen Halpern and Alison Hyde provided last minute help on several occasions, and I gained a lot from talking to Ruth Elliot. Finally I am especially grateful to Kathy Henderson who talked through many of the main arguments with me and provided enormous emotional and intellectual support.

CHAPTER ONE

The Basis of Health Care

Seldom has the National Health Service received more media coverage than it does today. Like all public services it has been affected by national economic policies designed to reduce the size of the public sector and yet it remains close to the hearts of most people in Britain and no political party likes to be seen to be seriously calling into question the quality of its provision. This makes it a peculiarly sensitive political creature. Reports of services closing or needs going unmet are immediately rejected by government spokesmen who produce a different set of figures to show that we have never had it so good. It is hard to discover where the truth lies.

On top of this, forty years of public health care have revealed serious shortcomings in the system and even before economics became the dominant influence on social policy, changes in thinking about health care and the way in which it is provided had begun to modify, if not significantly alter, the shape of the NHS.

Between them these different influences have generated a period of greater turmoil and change in the NHS than at any time since its inception. In the last decade the Health Serivce has been through two major administrative shake-ups, has lost half of its hospitals and has begun to lay the basis of a major reorganisation of its pattern of provision. Some services have totally disappeared, others have changed beyond recognition and yet others are being built up for the first time. In the midst of this upheaval it is extremely difficult to know where things are leading. Supporters say the service is immeasurably better; opponents say it has been butchered. This book attempts to sort out what is going on.

In the back of my mind as I write, is a phrase often repeated by government ministers when attacked for their record on the National Health Service: 'The NHS is safe in our hands'. Much circumstantial evidence appears to contradict this, and what does 'safe' mean at a time of rapid change? How do we judge the record of a government?

Various measures have been used to take the temperature of the National Health Service, but all are crude approximations and none translate well over time. One approach has been to look at the standard of health of a population on the assumption that health is a measure of health care, but there is no clear correlation between the two. Health is determined by a wide range of social and economic factors which reach far beyond the remit or control of any health care system and the standard of health of a population will tell us at least as much about the society as a whole as about the adequacy of its health care service. This does not mean that the NHS should pack up and go home, merely that it has to work in conjunction with a number of other influences.

To get around this, commentators have fallen back on indicators of the adequacy with which the Health Service deals with the health problems presented to it. But how do you measure adequacy? Can it be captured by quantifiable things like the number of hospital beds per head of population or the number of treatments performed in them? We know, for instance, that the number of people waiting for treatment in some of the more important medical specialties, and the length of time they spend waiting, has appreciably increased in the last twenty years. The number of people waiting for inpatient treatment has gone up from the half-million mark in the mid-1950s, to a peak of nearer three-quarters of a million in the early 1980s, dropping back slightly to around 600,000 today. We know that the length of wait has also increased.[1] But what does this tell us? Is it because fewer treatments are being performed, more people are getting ill, or because a greater variety of complaints are capable of treatment and people who in the past would have died or assumed that their complaint was inoperable, have joined the queue? In other words, has supply gone down or demand gone up? We know, in fact, that although the number of treatments being offererd in some parts of the country is being held back by financial constraints,[2] the NHS, overall, is performing more treatments, across a greater variety of complaints, than ever before in its history. But volume alone can hide as much as it reveals. We do not know whether the increased volume is partly made up by the same people coming back for further treatment because the first was unsatisfactory or whether increased hospital activity is related to failures elsewhere in the service which might have prevented the need for such treatment in the first place;[3] has hospital activity gone up because the preventive and community medical services have gone down? It is difficult enough to provide satisfactory answers to these questions today; it is impossible to provide them on a comparative basis over time – the indicators simply are not there.

Yet another approach is to look at levels of funding on the assumption that the better the funding, the more adequate the service. At one level this is self-evidently true, but only up to a point; it depends on how resources are used. As government spokesmen have repeatedly pointed out in recent years, there is no clear correlation between inputs and outputs and it would be naive to pretend that an organisation as large as the Health Service has not in the past, and does not still, contain areas where resources could be better used. This does not have to mean straightforward inefficiencies, though it may. An increase in funding may simply mean that more resources are put into sophisticated operations which have a very low success rate, or into new diagnostic procedures which produce questionable results. Neither are cost effective.

Part of the difficulty is that any assessment of adequacy needs to take account of the *kind* of treatment which is being provided. Is the NHS putting large sums of money into sophisticated diagnostic and treatment procedures when what most people need is somebody to talk to or when the big health issues of the day are a result of the kind of society we live in? In other words, no matter how much the NHS is doing, if it is doing the wrong things, or doing them in an inappropriate fashion, then it is still an inadequate service. Here we enter a large and fundamental debate about the nature of health care.

The National Health Service was grafted onto a health care system with very specific ideas about health and ill health. In particular it inherited a body of ideas which emphasised the centrality of the curative process: the idea that disease or ill health is a malfunction of a particular organ or part of the body and that the task of the health care professional is to diagnose the problem and repair it, rather like an engineer repairs a faulty machine. It raised cure above all else – prevention, care, human relations, and the wider society – and in doing so moved the medical profession to the centre of the health care stage, providing doctors with a powerful legitimising ideology which continues to underpin their power and prestige today. But it is a very partial model of ill health and therefore of health care. For many of us, much of the time, ill health is not a readily definable, mono-causal event, which can be attributed to a 'bug' or an easily diagnosable physical malfunction of a part of the body. An increasing amount of illness is being recognised as a *complex* of physical, psychological and environmental issues.[4]

It may be that the intolerable headache which we present to the doctor for treatment is simply a 'medical' manifestation of other concerns or pressures in our lives which probably have nothing to do with medicine or the Health Service. Barbara Stillwell, a pioneer in primary health care, tells the story of a woman who presented herself at a surgery complaining of backache. 'My back's killing me, I can't sleep and the kitchen ceiling has fallen down,' she complained.[5] It did not take a great deal of diagnostic skill to decide which was the most important and to call in a builder.

At a more complicated level there is a growing under-standing that some of the most serious diseases facing us today – cancer, mental illness and heart disease for instance – are physical manifestations of a complicated combination of causes which may also have environmental and psycho-logical origins. It follows that a model of disease which confines itself to locating the immediate, bodily, physical sources of the problem and coping with that, leaves whole areas of ill health undiagnosed and untreated. Such a model also tends to underrate the importance of the experience of being treated. If it is true that health care is only a sophisticated branch of engineering then the quality of the relationship between patient and health worker is relatively unimportant; it becomes a matter of fault-finding or diagnosis followed by repair or cure. The relationship can remain impersonal, even depersonalised. But if this is not true then the relatively straightforward procedure of physical diagnosis and cure becomes only one element in a broader curative process which demands an understanding of people and necessarily requires a fuller human relationship between patient and doctor. As we have come to understand more about the complex nature of disease and ill health, it has become apparent that the *quality of the experience of being treated* is often as important as the treatment itself in determining a successful outcome.

Traditionally it is common practice for the different areas of health care to be designated separately as the curing and caring services. Curing is what concerns doctors; it is what happens in most hospitals and has always been taken to be the most important criterion against which to judge the success of the service. Caring is what friends, relatives and perhaps lower status professionals like nurses do; it is about looking after people who have been 'cured' and are now recovering or who are, by definition, incurable. This is now understood as a largely false divide and any assessment of the adequacy of the Health Service must include a judgement about how successfully it is facing up to these new understandings and overcoming the initial bias of its origins. This is not to underrate the enormous advances that have been made in understanding the human body and curing some of its afflictions, or their importance. Many of these have revolutionised people's lives and will remain milestones in human progress forever. But medicine still does not equal health care; it is one component of it and to the extent that it has obscured other aspects it has arguably put back the advance of human health. A comprehensive health care system needs to move beyond the engineering analogy.

This too has to go into the weighing scales. But we have moved far beyond the easily quantifiable, and comparisons over time become even less meaningful. There are problems of information, definition and measurement which render comparisons virtually meaningless and even if we could muster all this material how would we weigh possible gains in one area against losses in another?

Adequacy turns out to be a difficult concept to pin down and measure. Are we therefore forced to conclude that no meaningful judgements can be made about the progress of the Health Service? It is important to know how it measures up against the base line of aspirations and needs it was originally established to fulfil, and which subsequent generations have internalised, taken for granted and made their own. They are perhaps the only meaningful marks against which it is possible to assess how adequately it is performing. What is this base line? The driving force behind the setting up of the NHS was a desire to provide a system of free, universal and comprehensive health care which would liberate people, as far as is possible, from the worry of illness and disability.

Behind this lay two main concerns: the first was a commitment to *equality* of access regardless of wealth, position or power; the second was a commitment to a *comprehensive* service which would cover the entire range of health needs and requirements. Together they represented the triumph of a body of ideas about the kind of society we wanted to live in. The notion that anybody could walk into a hospital and be cared for, no matter what their wealth or status, symbolised a set of values which emphasised equality, and care for others. For many it was more than merely an idly held belief: it was an essential part of a general sense of security and well-being. It represented the thin veil which protects us from some of the more grotesque indignities that human beings can impose on one another and made the world feel a safe place in which to bring up children and grow old.

There were, of course, problems from the beginning which undermined this simple aspiration. The NHS took over a body of voluntary, charitable and local government institutions which accurately reflected the divisions of wealth and poverty in the country at large and which were heavily biased in favour of the more prosperous areas. This bias, somewhat softened, is still with us. The NHS also inherited, as we have seen, a particular body of ideas about what constitutes good health care and the emphasis on curative medicine has not helped in the provision of a comprehensive service. It has down-graded the importance of providing services for people it considers, often correctly, cannot be cured so that many of the caring areas of the service, the long-stay hospitals for the mentally handicapped, or facilities for the elderly, have been starved of resources and still remain underprivileged.

It has further fostered a belief that demand for the Health Service is, by definition, insatiable and therefore funding can never be adequate. By down-playing the causes of ill health and emphasising their cure it has done nothing to

stem demand, while developments in the curative process
have continually increased the number of people who can
legitimately make calls on the service. Demand goes up and
up, regardless of funding. This, in turn, has provided every
government since the inception of the NHS with a perfect
excuse, if it needed one, for turning a blind eye to unmet
needs and ignoring substantial evidence that some parts of
the service have never been adequately funded, however
efficiently or inefficiently resources have been used. The
worst-funded areas are, of course, those furthest from the
curative process, but even hospitals devoted to curing
people are often shabby, decaying and inadequate.

Today the reality of the Health Service is some way from
the aspirations which lay behind its establishment. It has
been shaped and moulded by the economic, social and
political context in which it has grown up and this, it turns
out, has not always been very compatible with ideas of
equality, comprehensiveness and security. The challenge
which successive governments have faced is whether or not
to strive to nudge the service from its current reality towards
the original aspirations. This is the only meaningful measure
of success and adequacy.

Haringey

Much of the evidence used in this book is drawn from one
health district. I chose Haringey because it is where I live,
not because it is any more or less typical than anywhere
else. The value of focusing on one district is that it is possible
to look at the way in which political, economic, medical and
managerial pressures shape the different components of the
service – hospitals, clinics, GPs – and how these then mesh
together to produce the service we, the public, encounter. It
is only at the local level that changes in the different areas
work themselves out and can be judged in the light of the
adequacy of the total service they provide.

The disadvantage is that past traditions and different

patterns of provision and need mean that no two parts of the country start from the same position or are even moving in the same direction. They may face similar problems but they face them from different vantage points and in different ways. Some are better funded than others, some have more rapidly aging populations, some have a better GP service and others a more comprehensive local authority social service. On top of this, government policies designed to even out these differences are, far from homogenising the situation, at least at the moment, fostering very different experiences in different parts of the country. Some areas, traditionally better funded, face protracted contractions in their budgets and are being forced to slim down their services rapidly while others are still growing and expanding, albeit in a small way.

This said, it is possible to overstate these differences. The principal changes over the last decade in the administration and character of the Health Service are part of a rethink in national policy which is being expressly applied at a national level in an attempt to reduce local and regional variations. A national service is being imposed from above and local idiosyncrasies are tending to be overruled. In a broad sense much of what is happening in Haringey is echoed elsewhere and even where it is not, the local experience provides an insight into the *feel* of the National Health Service in the late 1980s.

Haringey is not a place, it is an administrative convenience which stretches across the north of London from the flat marshes of the River Lea in the east to the hills of Highgate and Hampstead Heath in the west. Up the middle runs the main railway line from Kings Cross to Scotland, chopping the borough in half in almost every important sense. The west is hilly and leafy; the east flat and densely built over. The west is comfortable and prosperous, the east uncomfortable and poor; the west is Conservative, the east Labour; the population of the west is predominantly white, while the east has one of the highest concentrations of ethnic minorities in any part of Britain. Two worlds with different histories, identities and interests and, although it is easy – and tempting – to overdraw the contrasts, they remain fundamentally different places, pulled uncomfortably together when the old London boroughs of Tottenham, Wood Green and Hornsey were merged in the reorganisation of local government in 1965.

The main roads, crossing north to south, reflect the contrived nature of the district; big arterial roads in and out of London. There is the Roman Ermine Street, built to link settlements on the Thames with Roman Lincoln, which still carves a more or less straight line up the middle of north London, though now rechristened Kingsland Road as it runs up through Hackney, becoming Stoke Newington High Street, Stamford Hill and Tottenham High Road. Slightly to the west there is the Great Cambridge Road, which, as the A10, runs up from Wood Green to Enfield, Hertford and eventually Cambridge, and further west still, the Great North Road, or A1, from London to Edinburgh. Few routes run east to west and those that do meander aimlessly through shopping arcades and residential streets, never meant to be more than byways; people have not much wanted or needed to cross from Tottenham to Highgate, or the other way around. So completely, in fact, does the railway sever the district in two that along its entire three-and-a-half mile length there are only four crossing points.

Highgate, perched comfortably on top of its hill and with commanding views of the rest of the borough, is rescued from suburban monotony by clusters of fine Georgian and early Victorian buildings and a 'village' high street. It has always been a desirable spot raised above the noise and fumes of the surrounding city. There are blue plaques commemorating the brief sojourns of Charles Dickens and A. E. Housman and a brass plate for the poet Samuel Taylor Coleridge who spent the last nineteen years of his life in 'the village', as some of its residents still like to call it.

Highgate Cemetery and its maze of terraces, winding paths, tombs and catacombs, some of the most celebrated and eccentric funeral architecture in Europe, falls down the southern slopes towards the centre of London, and Highgate public school, with its navy-blue blazers trimmed in maroon, lends to the village the air of a provincial cathedral town.

Near the centre stands the Highgate Literary and Scientific Institution, one of the few remaining private libraries in the country and a memento of the literary and scientific clubs which flourished in the 1830s. Notices pinned up in the entrance hall advertise a lecture on 'A day in the life of a publisher', a spring dinner for members – £9.50 per head including wine – and the Hendon and Hampstead Ceramic and Glass Club. It is quiet and empty in the reading room with a circle of chairs drawn up around an empty fireplace; pictures on the walls in thick frames, brass door fittings polished to a deep shine and a clock with a tick which marks the passing of time just a shade too quickly for comfort. There are tables laden with magazines ranging from the *Antique Dealer* and *Homes and Gardens* to the *New Statesman* and *New Scientist*. Outside, trees in Pond Square suggest a peaceful, almost rural outlook, belied only by the noise of home-bound rush-hour traffic snarled up in South Grove. The library boasts a collection of some 40,000 volumes with a bias towards biography, history and literature. The 'scientific' dropped out some years ago as the ideal of the educated Victorian gentleman who dabbled in science in the morning and literature in the afternoon, came up against the contemporary reality of funding a small private library and the difficulties of keeping abreast with the changing popula- tion and character of Highgate. A pamphlet written in the 1950s still maintained that the Institution was the 'axis around which the social and cultural life of Highgate Village rotates', and although it is doubtful whether it was true even then, it certainly is not today. But, with its air of history and exclusivity, the Institution continues to represent something of the spirit, if not the material reality, of the neighbourhood.

Posters pinned carefully to trees and fences advertise choral evenings, cats lost and found and avant-garde French films, but behind the main streets are roads of vast, detached houses often swapping hands for a million pounds or more; homes for the super-rich more interested in oil-wells and shipping lines than literature and science.

Beyond these and down the hill stretch the 'Highgate Borders', a surprisingly large area in estate agent parlance, reaching out towards Muswell Hill, Crouch End and Stroud Green, the old areas of Hornsey. They are solid middle class neighbourhoods with occasional pockets of poverty which gradually increase as you move east towards the railway lines and Tottenham. It remains hilly country and from Muswell Hill Broadway it is possible to catch glimpses, through the gaps in the buildings, of endless terraces of houses running down the flanks of the hills to Crouch End and up again the other side. Much of the area was thrown up by Victorian and Edwardian speculative developers who covered the wooded hillsides and small market gardens with homes for the middle classes during a thirty-year building boom around the turn of the century. Many of the streets are variations on the same Edwardian theme: red-brick houses with large windows, fancy woodwork, elaborately fretted and stained glass front doors and fancy wrought iron railings. Some are double-fronted, some single, others are on many levels to accommodate the steeply sloping sites; there are houses divided into as many as half-a-dozen flats and some are still large family houses.

The size and character of the buildings are not accidental. In the 1900s the local burghers of Hornsey viewed with horror the spread of working-class housing in neighbouring Tottenham and vowed that Hornsey should not go the same way. To this end the local authority insisted on wide tree-lined streets, proper sanitary arrangements and decent standards of building; it regularly pulled down jerry-built houses. In 1903 the council even published a pamphlet called *Healthy Hornsey* in which it described itself as a 'municipal borough within seven miles of Charing Cross and yet inhabited entirely by the middle class. Not a house without at least a little slip of garden in the front and a larger tract at the rear.'

The modern burghers of the Highgate Borders are no less fastidious about their environment and for some years the biggest single local issue has been a bitter battle with the Department of the Environment over plans to widen the Archway Road, part of the A1, turning it into a six-lane urban motorway and splitting the neighbourhood in two.

Meanwhile over in Tottenham, the talk in the local pubs and cafés is more likely to be of the quality of the local first division football team, Tottenham Hotspurs. The Spurs stadium stands in the middle of the area, half-way up the High Road and surrounded by its spin-off enterprises: the supporters' club and the souvenir shop. On match days the pubs for half-a-mile in each direction close and the hamburger and hot dog stalls are wheeled out, sending clouds of acrid, onion-laden fumes into the late afternoon air. Litter piles up in the gutters and the police line up on horseback in front of the main entrance, breaking up groups of rival supporters who mill around in the middle of the road, bringing traffic to a standstill. Tucked away in the side streets are vans of reinforcements and a specially equipped communications and surveillance van. Football violence is on everyone's mind.

Around the football ground, built on flat land bordering the River Lea, are rows of small terraced houses. James Dean, an early Victorian observer, toured the area in the 1830s, at about the same time as the Highgate Literary and Scientific Institution was built, and recorded: 'There is generally a malaria floating over the low, wet lands; when the stench of neglected drains mixes with it, fever and bowel complaints follow, especially among the poor.'[6] Reports in the 1850s talked of the housing accommodation for the poor being 'chiefly to be found in lanes, courts and alleys, without drains, ventilation or a supply of water and in addition much overcrowded'.[7] These fetid lanes have today been replaced by Victorian terraces, but profiles of the area, drawn up by the local authority, talk of a 'high proportion' of houses which still lack basic amenities like baths and inside toilets, and of the generally 'poor environment': narrow, cramped streets, unsightly derelict plots, large volumes of traffic and a shortage of open spaces. Some of the area has been redeveloped and replaced by large council estates, but many of these have problems of their own. Most are poorly maintained and some of the bigger, newer, high density ones have been a disaster almost ever since the day they opened. From the flats of the now notorious Broadwater Farm estate, opened in the 1970s, you can see across the district to the green slopes of Muswell Hill. But under them is a concrete wilderness of windblown galleries and semi-underground car parks, home for burnt-out cars and groups of unemployed teenagers. The estate was unpopular and feared long before the riots of 1985 and empty flats stud the serried ranks of concrete blocks.

Since the reorganisation of local government in London in 1965, there have been attempts to build Wood Green, which straddles the railway line and contains a little of Hornsey and Tottenham, but none of their extremes, into a new natural focus for the borough. It is a mixed, rather anonymous commuter dormitory which has never been either a safe Labour or Tory area. The new Haringey council built a modern shopping centre and hoped that it would break the shopping habits of a lifetime, but travel and transport from east to west is still less easy than on the north to south routes and Haringey remains a deeply divided borough – a microcosm of the extremes of the divisions in broader society.

These extremes do not show up very clearly in the data for economic and social well-being which are largely derived from census material and do not work well for small areas. But even the gross figures for the whole of Haringey suggest that, notwithstanding Highgate and its borders, the area suffers from serious social deprivation. The figures show that on five commonly accepted indicators of deprivation – single-parent families, overcrowding, lack of amenities, mobility and ethnic origin – Haringey features amongst the worst 10 per cent of boroughs in the country. In the case of ethnic minorities only two districts, west Birmingham and the London borough of Brent, have a higher overall proportion than Haringey and in 1980, the last figures available, 53 per cent of births in Haringey were to mothers born outside the UK. Unemployment is around 15 per cent, the seventh highest in London and some 5–7 per cent higher than the London average. A survey by the former Greater London Council of housing in the city found that Haringey contained some of the worst problems in London with an extreme housing shortage – 10,000 on the council's waiting list – a high proportion of households sharing basic amenities and one in seven houses 'unfit for human habitation'.[8] Since these figures average out extremes of wealth and poverty, it is fair to assume that the problems of Tottenham and the east end of the borough are substantially worse and small surveys by the local authority back this up. The council has long believed that the Tottenham area shares all the characteristics of inner-city deprivation found in more obviously deprived areas and has unsuccessfully appealed to successive governments for inner-city designation.

The social character of the area is one of several influences which have important implications for the Health Service. At a national level the most important is the growing proportion of the population which is dependent on other people for support in surviving and maintaining a decent standard of life. A large part of this figure is made up of an increase in the relative and absolute numbers of the old and very old. Received wisdom has it that at around the age of seventy-five people start to make heavy demands on the health and social services. This group has increased by over half-a-million in the last decade and the bulge is gradually working its way up through the age ranges so that there is an increasing proportion of very elderly infirm people.[9]

To this must be added the growing number of mentally and physically handicapped people who, ten or fifteen years ago, might have died at birth but who now, thanks to advances in medical understanding and treatment, survive into middle and even old age.[10] Between them these groups represent one of the biggest challenges facing the Health Service today.

Figures for Haringey show that the local population is aging less rapidly than the national average, probably because people of retirement age are leaving the area and being replaced by a new and more mobile younger group, but the figures for the elderly frail and infirm are still substantial. Statistics for mentally and physically handicapped people are less clear cut because they have not been fully kept in the past, but Haringey can expect to be catering for several thousand in the coming years.

An almost equally important challenge is highlighted by the growing body of evidence which shows that despite forty years of free public health care, there are still enormous inequalities in health in Britain which mirror the inequalities in wealth and income. A Department of Health and Social Security (DHSS) commissioned report in 1980, for instance, which looked at inequalities in health found that working-class men and women (occupational class 5) had a two-and-a-half times greater chance of dying before reaching retirement age than their professional counterparts in occupational class 1.[11] This suggests a strong relationship between social and economic conditions and standards of health. Local figures are sparse and limited and do not discriminate between the east and west of the borough. But they show that, as a whole, the infant mortality ratio, that is the ratio between children who live and die in the first twelve months of life, has fallen less rapidly in Haringey than in the country as a whole and is now marginally worse than the national average; the same is true for mortality figures for other age groups.[12] It is safe to assume that these figures have been heavily influenced by conditions in the east and mean that a district like Haringey needs to think hard about how it is going to provide an equal and comprehensive service for its enormously divided population. Perhaps it should mean positive discrimination in favour of the Tottenham area.

Haringey's health service is run by a district health authority. These are peculiar and unique organisations which bear no relationship to what we normally understand by a local authority. Our understanding of local authorities is coloured by what we know about the more familiar local councils. But councils are arms of local government and enjoy, through elected councillors, a small measure of autonomy to decide how to run their affairs. They control schools, housing, social services and roads but they do not control the health service. Haringey district health authority is an arm of the National Health Service, which is run by the Department of Health and Social Security. There is no formal local representation and a rapidly diminishing degree of local autonomy.

The NHS is a rigid, hierarchical pyramid. The government, through the DHSS, appoints fifteen regional health authorities covering England and Wales, which in turn appoint 192 district health authorities, although the Secretary of State for Health retains a tight grip on the whole process through powers to appoint the chairmen of all 207 'local' bodies. As a sop to local sensibilities these appointees are usually drawn from the local population; normally the local medical and nursing professions, voluntary organisations, trade unions, employers and local councils. They may informally uphold the interests of their nominating organisations, but they are in no sense formal representatives and many represent nobody except themselves – the local equivalent of the great and the good. The partial exception are local authority nominees who are usually councillors and to that extent subject to local pressures. But it is a system which has been deliberately designed to lift the Health Service out of the cut and thrust of local politics, a decision originally taken when the Health Service was set up in the 1940s and doctors strongly objected to being subordinated to what they saw as the whims of local politicians. To a large extent it has been very successful. Health authority members may not always agree among themselves, but political affiliations and local interests are only indirectly and often dimly felt and there have been very few instances indeed of a local health authority defying central government policy in the name of a local concern.

This distance between the local authority and the local health service is mirrored in an enormous discrepancy between their respective geographical boundaries even when they share the same name. Thus Haringey health district's responsibility for services is by no means as straightforward as its name implies. It is not responsible for GP or family doctor services, which are run by a completely different organisation with a different constitution and different powers, called the Enfield and Haringey family practitioner committee. Nor, even less logically, is it responsible for hospitals in the western half of the district which are run by various other London health authorities. Between them these take away a very substantial chunk of the local service and, as we will see, render the idea of planning a coherent *local* response to *local* needs pretty empty. Extraordinary as it may seem, there is no one forum which brings together the full range of statutory organisations responsible for providing health and welfare services in the geographical area of Haringey.

The health district is part of North East Thames regional health authority, a part of the country which has historically received more funds per head of population than anywhere else in Britain. It has one of the best ratios of hospital beds and hospital doctors per head of population in the country. Haringey has shared in this relative affluence although its hospitals, hidden away in depressed and forgotten areas of Tottenham, show few signs of this.

The district's main hospital, catering for the entire east of the borough, is called the North Middlesex. It is an old work-house hospital where the poor of Edmonton and north Tottenham once went to die. It has never shaken off the reputation of a second class, poor law institution. A planning document produced by the health authority talks of the 'unappealing mixture of building stock and styles', and describes the hospital as 'inefficient, in poor condition (and) with poor *functional* relations between the services'.[13] By this it means that many buildings are not linked to each other and to move a patient from a medical to a surgical ward, which happens quite often, or to take a medical patient for a comprehensive X-ray, means taking them outside and across a road. Small electric ambulances like boxed-in milk-floats transport those who are too sick or frail to walk or go by pushchair. Even so it is inefficient and inadequate with an enormous duplication of facilities: four or five X-ray departments scattered across the site, operating theatres in different buildings, all of which require their own back-up staff and facilities. Most serious of all, the accident and emergency department is at the far end of the complex and at least one patient, perhaps more, I was told, had died in the ambulance as it threaded its way through the hospital's one-way traffic system which gets badly clogged during the evening rush hour. 'Dynamite stuff,' the administrator admitted, though fortunately for the health authority it has never leaked out.

An appraisal of the hospital by a team of building consultants in the early 1980s recommended the demolition of the entire medical, surgical, X-ray, accident and emergency and intensive care departments, some 60 per cent of the hospital's buildings, as soon as possible. By the turn of the century this goal may have been achieved.

Four miles away in south Tottenham is St Ann's, the district's second hospital. It is an elderly, threadbare institution with a homely but forgotten feel. 'St Ann's, St Whose?', runs the self-deprecating joke. Gaunt Victorian ward blocks which except for a few coats of paint can have hardly altered since they were opened by the Metropolitan Asylum Board in 1892 as the North London Fever Hospital, run down one side of the site, linked by open corridors with cast-iron poles and glass roofs which, dimly lit at night, create the illusion of being in a Victorian time-warp. There have been new additions, notably in the 1930s when a series of two-storey red-brick ward blocks were put up by the London County Council which turned it into a general hospital, but since then time at St Ann's has virtually stood still.

If it stands still much longer it will quietly crumble away. It is hard to better the official description of the hospital, tacked on the wall of a corridor in the administrative block, which describes the Victorian wards as being virtually at 'the end of their useful life' and the newer 1930s wards as damp and unhygienic. 'Most buildings need extensive works and unless the deterioration on the new side can be halted the buildings may become beyond economic repair as is the case in the majority of the buildings in the Victorian part of the hospital.'

Between them these two hospitals absorb some 80 per cent of the district's budget, leaving precious little for other services. The district has traditionally ignored the special needs of the mentally ill and handicapped, there are scrappy and inadequate facilities for the growing number of elderly people, and non-hospital services like clinics and health centres are patchy and uneven.

It is a depressing catalogue of neglect for an area which is historically better funded than most parts of the country and raises doubts about the quality of the service elsewhere. Haringey should be an NHS showcase. Does it mean that even the most favourably funded parts of the Health Service may have been unable to adequately modernise and update their services on the funds they have been given, or has it merely made poor use of what it has had?

Recent governments have tended to conclude that while some parts of the country and some parts of the Health Service do indeed need extra cash, much of the problem can be attributed to poor administration and an inefficient use of funds. As a result, as the national economic situation has closed in and the political acceptability of providing more overall cash for the NHS has diminished, governments have tended to concentrate on issues of efficiency, value for money and managerial expertise. These preoccupations, along with pressures from the growing dependent population and reductions in public spending, have precipitated enormous changes. The rest of this book is an investigation into where this is taking us.

CHAPTER TWO

The New Managerialism

During the last decade the National Health Service has been through a period of unprecedented change and upheaval, greater than at any time since its foundation. The NHS of yesterday is unrecognisable from that of today, at least on the surface. It has moved from a period of growth to one of contraction. Nearly one third of the country's hospitals have been closed, from some of the very biggest to some of the smallest. It has been through two major reorganisations in about as many years which have transformed the way in which it is run. In the process it has radically reappraised its priorities; some services are disappearing, others are being created to take their place. But in all the upheaval two phases stand out as central for an understanding of the current state of the Health Service. The first starts in the mid-1970s and represents the dying throes of a period of expansion and hope. The second begins in the early 1980s and is symbolised by the emergence of a siege economy and a new body of managerial ideas. The two phases merge into each other, there was never a clear break and their separate contours are not always easy to discern, and yet they are characterised by very different ideas.

Phase one is a fulcrum period which marks the transition from the expansionist years of the late 1950s and 1960s, when there was still room to think about the big issues of public health and welfare, to the cutbacks in public spending which now dominate our thinking and have closed down the horizons, replacing bold plans with an emphasis on retrench-ment. Several years before this narrowing focus the Labour government of the day attempted to come to grips with some of the more obvious imbalances in the service which had been highlighted by the years of growth. Two imbalances in particular concerned it: an imbalance in the national distribution of resources to the different parts of the country and a parallel imbalance in the distribution of funds to the different components of the service. Between them they had created serious and quite large pockets of under-provision and under-funding.

But even as these programmes were taking shape, the growth in public expenditure began to fall and they were overtaken by economic pressures which undermined and distorted their potential for generating a fairer and more comprehensive service. For many people it was the end of a period of optimism. It was followed by years of growing concern about how to make ends meet in a period of financial restraint. Issues of managerial efficiency, perform-ance and accountability took over, culminating in 1983, when the Conservative government asked the managing director of the Sainsbury supermarket chain, Roy Griffiths, to refashion the National Health Service in the light of the new managerial emphasis. It was the beginning of what have become the managerial years; years which have transformed the operation of the Health Service and, in doing so, the character of the services it offers.

The NHS has never provided a very equal or compre-hensive service, but in the mid-seventies these issues were back on the agenda. The managerial take-over has immeasur-ably strengthened the hand of the Health Service's administra-tion and could have pushed this process further. But instead, at least temporarily, it has refashioned the service in its own image, turning it away from the broader aspirations and narrowing the focus to issues of administrative efficiency. In doing so it has come dangerously near to substituting means for ends.

It is not perhaps as straightforward as this makes it sound. In any organisation as large and complex as the NHS, changes are mediated through thousands of individuals and hundreds of circumstances. But it is important to understand the primary driving forces which are pushing it along. This chapter is about these forces and how they have changed.

The End of Optimism

In the late 1960s the Health Service still reflected many of the biases and distortions of its pre-NHS days. One of the most marked was the geographical distribution of resources. The pre-NHS service had been heavily influenced by the ability of the local population to pay and this had skewed it in favour of the more prosperous regions around London and the south east of the country. Twenty-five years later this pattern was still broadly unchanged. Some parts of England received 40 per cent more in health resources than the national average, measured in terms of hospital expenditure per head of population, whilst others received more than 20 per cent less. During the intervening years, funds had been distributed to the different parts of the country on the basis of demand for them, and demand was taken to be the requirements of the existing facilities for more. The system had built on, rather than challenged, the inequalities it inherited.

The first serious attempt to tackle this has been credited to the former Labour Health Minister Richard Crossman, who in 1970 introduced a formula designed to distribute money on the basis of a rough and ready measure of need for hospital beds. But five years later the national balance of health resources was still quite unacceptable. David Owen in his book *In Sickness and In Health* has recorded that in the mid-1960s expenditure per head on the hospital service in England varied from between £9.32 in the Trent region to £15.53 in the North East Thames region, a spread of over 50 per cent around the national average. In 1971–72 Trent was still bottom with £15.10 per head of population and North

East Thames was still top with £25.04, a percentage gap as great as before. By 1976–77, after several years of the Crossman formula, Trent was still bottom and North East Thames top, though the percentage gap had been reduced to a mere 36 per cent![1]

This was clearly not good enough and in 1974–75 the Labour government set up a DHSS study group known as the resource allocation working party (or RAWP for short) to look again at the distributive mechanism. The working party devised a formula, known as the RAWP formula[2], which, in theory, enabled it to measure the relative health needs of one population against another for the entire range of health provision. It did this by taking the number of people who live in an area or region and then, because people make differential demands on the Health Service, 'weighting' this population by age, sex, mortality, birth rate and marital status. Each of these is assumed to be an indicator of need. The very young and very old make more demands on the Health Service than those in between, men and women have different rates of use, mortality is a proxy for illness or morbidity, the birth rate is a measure of demand for antenatal and childbirth facilities, and marital status a crude proxy for deprivation and mental well-being. These weighted populations could then be used as the basis for determining the division of the NHS cake. However, since the existing division is badly skewed, it was deemed impractical to impose the full redistribution overnight. Both expansion and contraction take time and the weighted populations were therefore used to establish revenue allocation targets which the different parts of the country would gradually move towards over a period of years. The assumption was that both the targets and the speed of adjustment would vary with the annual size of the NHS cake, but whatever the national economic situation, there would be relative losers and gainers. Broadly speaking the formula meant that the London regions became relative losers and the northern regions relative gainers. North East

Thames region, which includes Haringey, was some 15 per cent above its target revenue allocation, or RAWP target, in 1976, closely followed by North West Thames, while Trent was some 10 per cent below.

The formula, first applied in 1976, still forms the basis upon which funds are distributed around the country, although during the intervening years it has been subjected to various criticisms. In particular mortality is a very questionable proxy for morbidity, or proneness to disease. Mortality statistics are based on death certificates and the immediate cause of death may be much less important, in Health Service, and quality of life, terms, than various chronic conditions which could have contributed towards it over a longer period of time — diabetes, smoking or alcohol addiction, for instance. These get lost in the formula which therefore has a tendency to underestimate demands arising from morbidity. The formula has also always been crude at measuring social deprivation even though this can have important effects on how people use the Health Service; how long they need to stay in hospital, for instance, or how able they are to articulate their needs. Lastly, RAWP excludes general practitioners (GPs) and family practitioner services although the quality and quantity of these can have a very substantial effect on the pattern of hospital usage.

Some of these criticisms have been taken on board and the formula modified. But the RAWP exercise was rapidly overtaken, within months of its introduction, by changes in the national economic climate which relegated these relatively detailed problems to the sidelines. In the first half of the 1970s the overall NHS budget had grown by an annual average of around 2 per cent in real terms; since the introduction of RAWP it has dropped to nearer zero. When RAWP was being put together nobody could have known that this would have been the long-term pattern. Two things have happened in the face of this squeeze: the progress of the regions towards their RAWP targets has slowed down so that the period of adjustment has been indefinitely extended and, more importantly, so-called above-target regions have become long-term net losers of revenue so that there can be small room for growth in the below-target parts of the country.

In 1976–1977 nine regional health authorities received growth allocations of up to 4 per cent, while five regions were held on no growth, in effect a cut when allowance is made for the impact of medical inflation and the growing number of elderly dependent people in the population, together estimated to be roughly the equivalent of about 1.5 per cent growth. Since then this pattern has been reproduced in succeeding years and in London and the south east of England, RAWP has become associated with cuts, something the original working party had never intended. The RAWP formula is, after all, only a method of measuring *relative* need and a crude measure at that; it has never pretended to be a measure of absolute levels of health need, although with cuts in some regions' budgets in the name of RAWP, this has become the predominant issue. It has meant that health districts like Haringey have become net losers of revenue in real terms since 1977.

The construction of the RAWP formula coincided with the publication of a second report in 1976 called *Priorities in the Health and Social Services*.[3] It was essentially a complementary exercise. While RAWP dealt with the gross distribution of the national cake to the different regions, the Priorities document looked at the distribution of funds *within* the Health Service to the different components that make it up.

The Priorities document was primarily an attempt to face up to the fact that future demographic projections suggested that the Health Service was heading for a major mismatch between demand for its services and the kinds of service it was offering. The vast bulk of resources were going into what is known as acute medicine – the services devoted to *curing* people, such as surgery, paediatrics and gynaecology – while the greatest future demand would be from people who were incurable and would therefore require long-term *care*. Population projections suggested a dramatic increase in the number of frail elderly people and in the number of chronically dependent mentally ill and handicapped people. Yet in 1976 the Health Service was devoting only 4.3 per cent of its resources to the mentally handicapped, 13.6 per cent to the care of the elderly and 7.5 per cent to the care of the mentally ill, and these last two figures included a certain amount of acute medicine. The worry was that if the NHS continued to pursue such a lopsided course of development, the mismatch of provision would be so great by the turn of the century that it would be unable to cope with the situation. It needed to broaden its base and increase the comprehensiveness of its cover. This could come either from an enlarged budget or from a readjustment of the service's traditional priorities. The Priorities document, alive to the gathering economic storm clouds of the mid-1970s, opted for the second.

It proposed a differential growth rate for different services; the long-term caring services or, as they became known, the 'priority services', would grow more rapidly than the rest. Services used mainly by the elderly were to grow at 3.3 per cent a year until the end of the 1970s, services for the mentally handicapped by 2.8 per cent and services for the mentally ill by 1.8 per cent, against an acute hospital rate of growth of 1.2 per cent, a drop in what had gone before of about 1.5 per cent.

At least as important as this, however, the document also proposed a shift in emphasis in the way in which dependent people are looked after and in doing so introduced the crucial notion of community as opposed to institutional care. Community care was not a new idea and perhaps because of this it is a difficult concept to tie down. It has meant different things at different times and to different groups of people. Judy Allsop, a writer and lecturer on social policy, has produced a neat summary of the problem.[4] She suggests that the primary idea behind community care is that individuals should be maintained in their homes wherever possible rather than in long-stay institutions. She argues that the idea goes back to the 1950s and has meant at least three different things:

1. Services provided in residential but relatively 'people-centred' and open settings
2. Services provided through the placing of professional and specialised personnel in the community
3. Services provided by the community on a voluntary or informal basis.

She suggests that during the 1950s and 1960s the emphasis was on the first two. In Health Service terms this meant services like day hospitals, district nurses and health visitors, while for the social services it meant day centres, meals on wheels, aids and adaptations to people's homes, social work support and home helps – all services designed to support dependent people in their own houses.

Behind this thinking was the work of groups of carers – doctors, nurses, social workers and volunteers – who were able to observe daily life in the large institutions and were becoming aware of the now well-known and documented syndrome of 'institutionalisation'. They argued that most chronically sick and handicapped people who needed long-term care would benefit from, and prefer to be looked after in, less institutional settings, preferably in their own homes but, failing that, in as close an approximation to home as possible, where they would be more likely to see friends and relatives and less likely to be anonymous numbers. There were pioneering experiments in looking after heavily dependent people in small community homes, as they were often called, which were usually ordinary houses converted into bed-sitters or hostels. In some cases the levels of medical, social and psychological dependency dropped appreciably and patients, or residents as they became known, appeared to live happier and fuller lives. These experiments, what is more, with their often optimistic-sounding conclusions, contrasted sharply with the over-whelmingly hopeless and demoralising tenor of reports emerging at the time from inquiries into some of the long-stay hospitals. These suggested chronic problems of funding, facilities and nursing care. They talked of 'old-fashioned, unduly rough and undesirably low standards of nursing', 'casual attitudes to death' and 'dismally and wholly in-adequate' facilities.[5] The Priorities document fed into this thinking.

However, its reasons for doing so may not have been entirely humanitarian. The document was acutely conscious of the economic backdrop against which it was reporting and concerned about where money would come from to develop the services it had highlighted. With the national NHS budget virtually static, would there be room for the differential growth rates it had proposed? Some money would come from the long-term relative shift in resources from acute medicine into the priority sectors, but this would take time, and might not be enough. The report recommended what it called 'new low cost' forms of health provision and under this category it appears to have included community care. It was careful not to be too explicit about the relative costs of community versus institutional provision and, although it argued that community care might provide better value for money, it did not say specifically that community care was a cheaper way of looking after people. But the suggestion was there, not least because it also called for the greater involvement of volunteer carers, to some extent no more than a recognition of the existing situation in which many dependent people are already heavily reliant on informal networks of families and friends.

In a less than totally honest fashion the Priorities document implied a shift in emphasis from paid institutional care and carers to unpaid, voluntary care and carers as a prerequisite for the country being able to look after its dependent population. Community care came to mean, in some instances, services provided by the community on a voluntary or informal basis, the third of Allsop's definitions. It is not the first time that the community approach has appeared to be both the humanitarian and cheaper option. A government report in the 1950s recommended that health policy should 'aim at making adequate provision wherever possible for the care and treatment of old people in their homes. The development of the domiciliary services for this purpose will be a genuine economy measure *and also* a humanitarian measure enabling old people to lead the sort of life they much prefer'.[6] (Emphasis added.) It was probably inevitable that this equation should raise its head again in the financially constrained 1970s when such a happy coincidence was bound to be a winning combination.

At the time, the implications of this new emphasis on the caring services for acute medicine remained a little uncertain. The Priorities document suggested that it might feel the pinch and proposed 'that there should be a particularly searching examination of the use of resources in these services with the aim of releasing resources for developments within the acute services themselves and for other hospital services, particularly geriatric medicine and mental illness'. It suggested that very significant savings could be made by rationalising hospitals, and that by cutting down the length of stay in them the Health Service could save in the region of £26 to £40 million, though it didn't explain the assumptions behind these figures. But a year later, as the Health Service's economic plight continued, this was firmed up. In 1977 the Labour government published a follow-up report called *The Way Forward*,[7] which modified and developed the previous planning guidelines in two significant ways. First it abandoned the growth targets outlined in the Priorities document. 'They are not specific targets to be reached by declared dates in any locality,' it wrote and explained that they were merely indicators of a general change in direction. Secondly it explained that the rationalisation of acute medicine was now the key 'upon which the rest of the national strategy depends', and it published for the first time guidelines suggesting target levels of bed provision and throughput per bed for acute medicine. It recommended an average of 2.8 acute beds per 1,000 people, against a current national average of about 3.4, and that throughput should be increased from a national average of 24.3 cases per bed per year to 28.2.

The guidelines were no more than informal guesses of what might be possible, based on what some authorities were achieving. Nevertheless they rapidly became the benchmarks against which all local health authorities were expected to plan their hospital services and, with a benchmark which suggested that many parts of the country were 'over-provided' with hospital beds, it became possible to legitimate stand-still, even negative, budgets. 'Over-provided' health authorities could be expected to take money out of their acute services and put it into the priority services which would then be able to grow in line with government policy, without an increase in overall spending. If the district was very 'over-provided' it could even do this on a falling budget.

The combination of tight budgets and the new policy provoked a major rationalisation of acute hospitals which was reflected in a dramatic increase in hospital closures. Between 1969 and 1974, 121 hospitals closed in England and Wales; between 1976 and 1978 this figure leapt up to 143 closures or 'changes of use', an expression which usually meant turning an acute hospital into a long-stay one for the elderly.[8] In the RAWP-losing London districts, this process was even more marked. Acccording to one calculation, London lost 26 hospitals between 1968 and 1975, a further 26 between 1975 and 1977 and a further 75 between 1977 and 1979.[9]

These figures do not, of themselves, invalidate the positive potential contained in both RAWP and the Priorities document. The Priorities document at least initiated a discussion about how the NHS was spending its money in service terms and, in so doing, challenged the automatic assumption that the bulk of the resources should continue to be channelled into curative services. But this should not be overstated. It is arguable that the Priorities document allowed itself to be distorted by economic imperatives in its deliberations about the caring services and so became the progenitor of a model of 'caring on the cheap' which has beset the caring services ever since. There is a sense in which it appears to have started out to challenge the intellectual traditions which have dominated health care, the automatic priority of the curative model of health care, but then 'bottled out' in the face of the implications of what it was saying. To get its message across it needed to call for either a substantial increase in funds or a substantial decline in acute medicine. But it seems to have found both so unpalatable that it ended up cheating on the services it was designed to help. Meanwhile the RAWP formula continues to ensure a more equitable distribution of funds across the country, but at the price of an extremely severe financial crisis for the RAWP-losing areas. It may be that the thinking behind the inception of these reports was right and sensible, but their outcome has fallen far short of what might have been achieved. They have come to represent a missed opportunity. They have been overtaken by the squeeze on public spending and this has vastly outweighed any benefits they might have produced. From being shapers of policy they have become shapers of the squeeze. This, certainly, is how it has appeared to the people of Haringey.

*   *   *

In 1977 Haringey's health budget fell for the first time in thirty years. Two years later the local community health council reported that the financial squeeze had become so severe that the district had been forced to temporarily close around 200 of its acute hospital beds in order to make ends meet.[10] It was not a long-term way to run a health service. But the district's plan to save money by rationalising its hospital beds had run into strong local opposition and a relatively weak and ineffectual management had been unable to force it through.

The plan envisaged the closure of four of the district's six hospitals, reducing the number of acute and semi-acute beds from 900 to 500. A planning document explained: 'The principle that underlies the strategy for the hospital service is that in a position of annually declining revenue, the district can only stay with its revenue allocation and also release revenue for priority services by rationalising acute services . . . the aim must be to maintain both the real quality and quantity of acute services yet provide these in the most efficient way so that resources are released for the under-provided priority groups.'[1]

Three of the four hospitals were specialised and relatively small: a thirty-eight-bed maternity hospital, a small cottage hospital used by GPs and a ninety-bed geriatric hospital. But the centrepiece of the strategy entailed the closure of the Prince of Wales, Tottenham's main local hospital.

The Prince of Wales is a fine mock-Georgian red-brick building which stands grandly in the middle of Tottenham, set back from the High Road behind tall railings and a small green. It had been Tottenham's local hospital for as long as anybody could remember and its façade is peppered with commemorative stones which mark the opening of a new ward or an additional wing – solid symbols of local pride and concern. Indeed, as a voluntary hospital in the pre-NHS days, it had been partly built and run on donations from the local population. Generations of families had naturally and automatically turned to it when they needed treatment and there can scarcely be anybody in the area who does not know somebody who has been treated there. It was everybody's idea of a local hospital: familiar, intimate, small and trusted, slap bang in the middle of the community and close to the shops and buses.

Ironically it was some of these very attractions which rendered it unsuitable in the eyes of the local administration. They saw it as small and cramped with little potential for development compared with larger neighbouring hospitals in the district. Three miles north stood the much larger North Middlesex with more beds, more specialties and more space. The people of Tottenham have never taken it to their hearts but with its large and extensive, albeit run-down, facilities, it was inconceivable that it could be closed down. Two miles south was St Ann's, home for many of Tottenham's long-term, elderly patients and with twice the bed capacity of the Prince and substantial scope for redevelopment. For the local management the choice seemed to make itself; the Prince was the obvious place to be shut down.

Moreover, other processes were at work which were gradually undermining the viability of small, acute hospitals like the Prince. The sheer cost and capacity of much modern medical technology has a centralising and concentrating influence. It is expensive to buy and run and often has an enormous appetite for work. A multi-channel auto analyser such as is used in modern pathology labs is able to perform ten to twenty different biochemical tests in virtually one operation. It doesn't make economic sense to install one in a hospital where it is not used to the full. Yet without the latest technology small hospitals are seen to be, and may actually become, second class institutions. This is certainly a view common among doctors, most of whom are inextricably wedded to the belief that 'good medicine' can only be practised where the very best and latest equipment is available and that to work anywhere else is to practise what one called scathingly 'second class medicine'.

During this period the Prince of Wales was also hitting severe staffing problems at junior hospital doctor level. Junior doctors provide much of the basic medical care in a hospital. But both juniors and their supervising authorities – most junior hospital doctors are in training – look for work situations which provide the trainee with a broad range of experience, a good medical library and time off to study. For some years the Prince had been failing to meet these criteria. St Bartholomew's medical school in central London, which

provided many of the basic raw recruits for the Prince of
Wales, had become an increasingly unreliable source of
supply. 'We would find that Barts would be coming to us
each year and saying "we're sorry, but we don't seem to
have any pre-registration students for you this year," '
explained Clive Amos, who at the time was an administrator
attached to the Prince. He remembers that the periodic
inspections by the Royal Colleges, which supervise more
advanced trainees, to ensure that the hospital offered
adequate training facilities had become nail-biting occasions
during the late 1970s: 'At each inspection we were on
tenterhooks; are we going to be able to persuade them that
this is a viable unit? It was always an open question and the
point at which they pulled the plug on us was never far
away.' Pulling the plug meant withdrawing support from the
hospital as a viable training establishment and this, in turn,
would have meant no junior staff, which would be the kiss of
death for a hospital practising acute medicine.

On top of this, hospitals suffer if they cannot offer their
junior staff reasonable working hours. Hospital medicine
works at two levels: the routine daily care of inpatients and
outpatients which can be broadly anticipated and scheduled
and, on top of this, unpredictable emergency work which
occurs at any time and necessitates, above all else, night
duty. It has always been the job of junior medical staff to
provide this cover and, during the 1960s and 1970s, it was not
uncommon for them to work eighty hours or more a week.
During the 1970s the DHSS began to encourage health
authorities to reduce these hours by cutting the pattern of
work from one night in two on duty to one night in three.
But for small hospitals like the Prince this reduction created
serious problems; it required a 50 per cent increase in staff to
maintain the same service and the health authority could not
afford this. On the basis of Department of Health guidelines,
small hospitals did not have sufficient beds to warrant the
extra staff. A small hospital like the Prince of Wales, with
under 200 beds, would normally have about forty beds per

medical specialty. Manpower guidelines suggested this was about sufficient to keep two junior medical staff busy, but not three. Thus Haringey could not afford to implement the one in three rota at the Prince and this, regardless of its other facilities, made it increasingly unattractive to junior medical staff, who in the late 1970s and 1980s could still pick and choose where they worked. The hospital was frequently under-staffed.

For the local management the problems seemed insurmountable and the logic of their solution overwhelming. A combination of the nature of medical training and prevailing economic policy was pushing the Prince of Wales into an ever more untenable position; the hospital was locked into a spiral of decline and the best thing was to close it, and sooner rather than later.

The local population, however, did not agree. They did not accept the government's budget restrictions and to some extent they did not accept the medical profession's commitment to bigger and more centralised hospitals. 'We are not of the opinion that, when it comes to hospitals, big is beautiful,' recorded the campaign group which sprang up to defend the hospital. 'The welfare of the patients, not administrative convenience, should be the criterion.' Among those involved in the defence campaign there was a certain incredulity that anybody could even contemplate Tottenham having too many hospitals. It did not square with their experiences of waiting for a bed or queuing for attention at the casualty department. 'The district health authority pretends that the work load will somehow either go away or be covered elsewhere. This is clearly impossible and it's little wonder that local people are disillusioned with the DHA's performance and have no confidence in its approach,' wrote one campaign document dismissively. 'There is already a shortage of beds at the North Middlesex to cover its present casualty department – if the Prince of Wales is closed where will the extra beds be found?'

The idea of losing the '*local*' hospital sent tremors through many of the district's older or less mobile residents. Like the man I met sitting in a wheelchair in the sun outside the Prince of Wales one morning. He said he lived half a mile away and once a week pushed himself to the Prince's physiotherapy department, which was temporarily maintained after the hospital closed because there was nowhere else to put it. Crossing the streets was a nightmare, but he knew every nook and cranny of the route; he knew where the pavement was broken up, where there was a ramp down into the road and how long he had to cross when the traffic lights on the High Road turned to red. He could have gone by ambulance, but ambulances never come on time and he treasured the freedom and independence of being able to take himself. But the imminent removal of the service to the North Middlesex or St Ann's was about to take this away from him. Some people at the time went further and swore that the proximity of the Prince had saved their lives. 'I was taken ill with a heart attack and within minutes I was in the (Prince's) casualty ward on a machine. If I had had to go to Edmonton (where the North Middlesex is) with the traffic jam, I might not be alive today,' recorded one. Rightly or wrongly, the closure of the Prince reduced people's confidence not just in the ability of the NHS to look after them, but in their perception of its desire to do so. The North Middlesex is a half-hour bus ride up the traffic-cluttered High Road from the centre of Tottenham and then a brisk ten minute walk. But in a gut sense the inadequacy or inconvenience of the alternative hospitals was not the issue. Hospitals are symbols of the NHS and the NHS is an expression of the degree to which we live in an equal and caring society. For forty years the welfare state has represented all that is best about our society and during these years we have put up with its failings and shortcomings, and continued to believe in it, because it embodied our wish to live in a safe and secure society in which we felt cared for and in which ill health is not a crippling financial or social disaster. We do not need to know whether a hospital is good or bad, or even what goes on in it; it is enough to know that it is there.

Against this set of values it is hard to see a hospital closure as in any way positive. Politicians may tell us that it is part of a restructuring and modernisation of the Health Service, but it does not feel like that. A hospital goes and nothing appears to take its place; how can it be seen as anything other than a diminution of the service and the destruction of one of the most important and cherished institutions we have created since the last war? In vain were the people of Tottenham told that the North Middlesex and St Ann's would be revamped to accommodate the services removed from the Prince; it felt like a step backwards. 'There is a widespread opinion locally that the district health authority plan is a document of expediency which seeks merely to react to circumstances rather than to put forward a convincing new health programme to meet the needs of the people of Haringey,' wrote the defence campaign. 'We believe Haringey is being stripped of its NHS assets.'

To add insult to injury, because the Health Service is not accountable or easily accessible to local opinion, there is a powerful sense of it being run by a team of bureaucrats, usually faceless, and government sycophants who cannot conceivably have the best interests of the local population at heart. In reality some may and some may not, but in their remoteness from the machinery of local politics it is almost inevitable that all health authorities and their members are seen as something other than the local community and this distance adds fuel to their opponents. There is a measure of truth in this, moreover. The conflict over the fate of the Prince represented an almost head-on clash of values between a group of administrators with no tradition or conviction that it was their business to challenge government policy and who accepted the need for greater productivity in the NHS, and a local population for whom a hospital symbolises their health service and to some degree all that is best and most important about the welfare state. To

Haringey's administration it was a question of seeking to manage a system they perceived as badly out of kilter with its goals. Between them RAWP and the Priorities document dictated a particular pattern and distribution of resources and services. They believed that the managerial challenge lay in running the system to comply with these demands. It was not their business to challenge their validity. The local opposition started from a totally different perspective; it did not accept the parameters as given and based its case on the expressed and perceived needs of the community. RAWP and the Priorities document did not come into it except as instruments which threatened the quality and quantity of the local service.

The opposition campaign rolled on for six months, gradually moving up the DHSS appeals machinery until it finally reached the Secretary of State for Health, Gerard Vaughan. Initially he approved the administration's plan, but then events took an unexpected turn. Within months of approving the plan, Vaughan made a tour of the district to see what the fuss was about, and after a morning looking round declared, to the amazement of the local management and the euphoria of the opposition, that the closure of the Prince of Wales would be frozen. The Conservative government was about to reshuffle the NHS administration and Vaughan decided that Haringey's plan should be reconsidered by the new local management. The local campaign saw it as a famous victory, which to some extent it was; it is quite unusual to be able to get the Minister of Health to step in and stop, albeit temporarily, a hospital closure. But in the longer term the victory was bound to be uncertain. The temporary stay of execution had frozen an increasingly untenable and unstable position and the new administration, introduced a year later in 1982, rapidly concluded that it could not be allowed to last.

The Management Years
The Conservative Party entered the 1979 election campaign

brandishing a commitment to slash the size of public bureaucracy and reduce government interference in the life of the country. The Party's central document on the National Health Service, published as soon as it gained office in 1979, was called *Patients First*[12] and committed the new government to streamlining the administration of the Health Service and devolving power from the centre to the periphery. It envisaged cutting out a tier of administration, reducing the number of tiers from four to three (see diagram below) and beefing up the power of the districts to run their own shows within broad national parameters.

But even as the plans were being drawn up, embarrassing questions began to be asked about whether the government really knew what was happening in the NHS. Opposition politicians challenged government ministers to demonstrate that their tight money policies were compatible with maintaining the standard and quality of the service. This the DHSS found hard to do; it had neither the information nor the information systems which would provide it with convincing and satisfactory answers.

More damagingly, a number of widely publicised reports

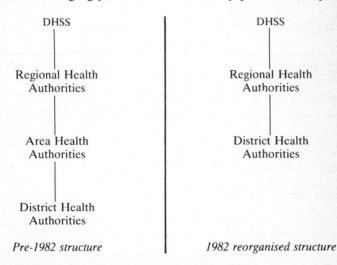

DHSS

Regional Health
Authorities

Area Health
Authorities

District Health
Authorities

Pre-1982 structure

DHSS

Regional Health
Authorities

District Health
Authorities

1982 reorganised structure

CHANGES IN NHS ADMINISTRATION

by House of Commons committees of inquiry seriously questioned the performance of the NHS, and its lack of accountability to the government and ultimately the tax payer. The House of Commons Public Accounts Committee in particular, questioned whether the NHS could deliver value for money and could combine substantial devolution with adequate accountability to parliament. Such doubts could not be ignored by a government which was committed, above all else and certainly above devolution of the NHS, to a policy of controlling public expenditure and ensuring that the public services provided the best possible value for money.

It found itself caught in the middle; it could neither defend itself from criticisms that the NHS was profligate nor from those that its economic policies were damaging the quality of the service. Gradually and without ever admitting it, ministers began to back-track on their commitment to devolution and only months before the formal introduction of the new structure, scheduled for April 1982, the DHSS issued a planning circular to health authorities which effectively faced in the opposite direction. It required the new district health authorities to submit annual plans to their appropriate regional authority which would combine them into a regional plan to be scrutinised by the Minister of Health himself. It was a new departure, imposing a planning hierarchy which had not previously existed. It was hard to square this with talk of devolution, and government ministers conceded that there was an 'apparent conflict' between the objectives of the 1982 reorganisation and the new planning guidelines.

They attempted to minimise the size of this 'U' turn by suggesting that greater freedom at district level naturally brought greater needs for accountability with it and that the new ministerial review procedure, as it was called, was merely the formal expression of this. But for district authorities it became a Trojan horse; it established new and firmer lines of accountability to ministers, through the DHSS and regions to districts, and once these were laid down, districts gradually found their freedom of manoeuvre confined to control over day-to-day decisions, while the larger and more important ones, which set the terms of these day-to-day decisions, were taken elsewhere. Devolution of power became increasingly hollow.

Moreover, the circular was followed by a stream of others which offered instructions, requests and exhortations to district health authorities to improve productivity and increase the value for money they were getting from their services. Gradually the circulars began to impose a new set of priorities on the Health Service: what it should value and what it should do. The new priorities emphasised the enormous importance of *management* and the value of introducing management tools which had long been employed in business and commerce. It is impossible to overstate the importance of these developments and their impact on later events. 1982 became, with hindsight, the year when management and managerial preoccupations took over the NHS and began to set the parameters within which we now think about public health care. While publicly the major change in the Health Service was the formal administrative reorganisation broadly outlined by *Patients First*, bigger and longer lasting changes were coming from a different direction. At a time of economic hardship, the vocabulary of management became the universal language of Whitehall and better management the key to solving the problem of resources.

It was only a matter of time before somebody was asked to pull it all together and in 1983 the government invited Roy Griffiths, managing director of Sainsburys, to look again at the entire administration of the NHS, but this time with the benefit of the new managerial enlightenment. The Griffiths team recommended yet more changes.[13] These were accepted by the government in March 1984 and implementation began later that year.

The Griffiths report was essentially a crystalisation of what was already happening. For a brief, even terse, report it contained much rhetoric about the need for 'developing managers', 'sharpening up the management process' and developing a more 'purposeful and coherent' style. Much of the problem was attributed to a lack of clear lines of authority and clearly identifiable chiefs. In a famous phrase it wrote: 'If Florence Nightingale were carrying her lamp through the corridors of the NHS today, she would almost certainly be searching for the people in charge.' The NHS administration, up until this point, had been based on a concept of team management; districts and regions were run by district and regional *teams* of officers drawn from the different areas of the Health Service – administration, nursing, finance and medicine – who met and took decisions on the basis of reaching a consensus. The assumption had always been that the different professions that make up the Health Service required a degree of autonomy: an administrator could not tell a doctor what to do any more than a nurse could tell a treasurer, and voting would therefore risk stepping on professional toes. Griffiths strongly disagreed. The inquiry team argued that consensus management was slow, produced decisions based on the lowest common denominator and failed to identify clear lines of responsibility. In particular it allowed doctors enormous freedom and as the main consumers of resources, made them the de facto controllers of the budget. The inquiry team wrote that the absence of an overall general manager meant 'that there is no driving force seeking and accepting direct and personal responsibility for developing management plans, securing their implementation and monitoring actual achievement'. It said that coming from a business environment it was surprised to find that 'rarely are precise management objectives set; there is little measurement of health output; clinical evaluation of particular practices is by no means common and economic evaluation of those practices extremely rare. Nor can the NHS display a ready assessment of the effectiveness with which it is meeting the needs and expectations of the people it serves. Businessmen have a keen sense of how well they are looking after their customers. Whether the NHS is meeting the needs of the patient and the community, and can prove that it is doing so, is open to question'. It recommended the abolition of team management and the establishment of general managers throughout. The concept was extended to the lowest level of the managerial hierarchy, even to hospital wards. The idea was that each area of activity would have a single, readily identifiable supremo whose task would be to run that area as tightly and efficiently as possible. Each manager was charged with the task of fostering better financial control, developing clearer planning guidelines and targets and vastly improving the monitoring and reviewing of performance against these goals.

The team was clearly aware that it might be criticised for introducing business techniques into a non-business environment. 'We have been told that the NHS is different from business in management terms,' it wrote, 'not least because the NHS is not concerned with the profit motive and must be judged by wider social standards which cannot be measured. These differences can be greatly overstated. The clear similarities between the NHS management and business management are much more important.' The transformation of the NHS administration, begun in 1982, was complete. Business management had taken over.

In the lead-up to the implementation of the Griffiths proposals in late 1984 there was much debate about the pros and cons of consensus management and the practicalities of subordinating the different professions, particularly the medical profession, to an overall management structure which might have very little medical expertise. But arguably the concept of consensus management was never much more than a sop to the professional pride of doctors, and to a lesser extent nurses, and its removal no more than an indication of the relative decline in influence of the medical profession in the overall running of the Health Service. In as much as their unique freedom of manoeuvre has long been an historical anachronism, this may be no bad thing.

Much more importantly, the single greatest achievement of Griffiths and its precursors has been to thrust management and management preoccupations to the very centre of NHS thinking. Management ideas now provide the dominant intellectual framework within which the Health Service thinks about itself and its role in society. They have begun to foster a regime in which particular kinds of activity are valued while others are pushed to one side.

What sort of ideas and activities take precedence? Modern management is about establishing systems in which activity can be measured against clearly defined objectives. It involves breaking down an activity into clearly understood inputs and outputs and developing procedures for monitoring and controlling this activity against agreed targets. It sounds innocent enough but it contains within it a very distinct set of values and assumptions. We can examine these through some of the issues which have become central to the running of the NHS today.

Performance

Managerialism emphasises the importance of developing measures of performance. There is no point in developing sophisticated procedures for monitoring and controlling an activity if you cannot measure it in the first place. But how do you measure health or health care? Management techniques have been developed in a business and commercial environment where activity can be clearly and straightforwardly broken down into readily definable components. The difficulty with introducing it into the NHS is that health care is not so readily quantifiable.

The DHSS set up a working party to look at how the NHS might do this in 1982. It was asked to develop a range of activity or performance indicators which would allow managers to judge how effectively the service was operating; how well it was using its resources and what it was getting out of them. The working party, a mixture of academics, civil servants and NHS managers, reported the following year with a package of performance indicators, or PIs, covering some of the more obvious and easily quantifiable areas of the NHS. They looked at how long patients stayed in hospital, how many patients used a bed in any one year, how much it cost to treat them and how much it cost to launder the sheets, and used these figures to compare the relative performance of different hospitals and districts. The figures allowed a district to look at its own performance over this narrow range of activity, and to compare it with those of others who might be doing better or worse. It enabled managers to ask why their laundry bills were higher than somebody else's or why one hospital appeared to be treating twice as many patients per bed as another. Everybody admitted they were a crude first stab at the problem, a starting point rather than a 'league table' of good and bad managers. Indeed it has been suggested that in compiling this first package of PIs the DHSS 'grabbed data out of the air' to quell growing criticism of its failure to adequately monitor the NHS's performance.[14] The argument went that they would at least allow managers to compare performances and identify areas which might warrant further investigation.

Since then the exercise has been extended to cover many more activities in the belief that the greater the detail in which activities are understood, the easier it will be to pinpoint potential sources of inefficiency. A second, much larger package of PIs was introduced in 1985 and another in 1986. Figures are now available for each health district covering hundreds of areas of activity and the system has been put onto computer discs so that administrators can punch up their relative performances.

But despite their widespread use, performance indicators are flawed by serious conceptual problems. Their primary value is confined to measuring readily quantifiable inputs and outputs while much health care is about qualitative

issues. It is of limited use to know how many patients pass
through a hospital bed in one year if you do not know the
outcome of their treatment. Activity does not necessarily
equal beneficial activity and PIs put us in the difficult
position of being unable to say whether an increase in
activity is actually improving the nation's health. Rudolf
Klein, Professor of Social Policy at Bath University and a
prominent commentator on the Health Service, has written
of this problem: 'The understanding of efficacy, effectiveness, efficiency and expenditure by different disciplines and
how these notions fit quality, make the business of measuring
any of these issues exceedingly difficult. Even the quite
simple comparison of input, process and outcome is confused by having to cope with the complexities of different
environments and differing levels of need and demand.'[15]

The PI working party has accepted much of this criticism.
In 1985 it admitted 'much needs to be done to develop PIs
and in particular to produce measures of adequacy, access
and quality of service. A start needs to be made now on
developing outcome measurements which could relate to the
effect of treatment'.[16]

These shortcomings underline the importance of not
taking PIs too seriously. Yet the thrust of NHS thinking,
under the influence of its new managerial values, has been to
give them a weight and substance far beyond their essentially
experimental nature; from being guidelines to how different
parts of the NHS are performing they are becoming
something dangerously close to tablets of stone. Even as
early as 1983, there were reports of the DHSS using them to
'cajole' health authorities into bringing services into line
with national averages,[17] and more recently ministers have
quoted them approvingly to point to increased productivity
in the Health Service – more people treated in fewer beds
than ever before – without questioning whether this increase
has been beneficial to patients. DHSS figures for 1986 show
that the number of inpatient treatments rose by 15 per cent
between 1978 and 1984, while the number of hospital beds

fell by over 17,000. These show, government ministers have told us, that health authorities 'are identifying ways of doing their jobs more effectively'. But do they? What they do not tell us is whether the reduced length of stay in hospital merely means that more people are being forced to return for second and even third visits. In other words, they do not tell us whether more people or more patients are being treated.

It is not just a question of what is not being measured; the process of emphasising the importance of being able to measure activity tends to value certain kinds of health care over others. A good doctor is one who maximises his or her measurable activity. Health care becomes associated with the number of activities performed: the number of patients treated, the number of operations carried out or the number of drugs dispensed. In so doing, the new management ideology reinforces a model of health care in which patients are treated as a series of discrete operations, each of which can be quantified and costed and each of which has a precise outcome. The quality of the overall process, or the experience of treatment, disappears. The patient/doctor or patient/nurse relationship comes down to something which can be measured in terms of what is done. There are no bonuses for the doctor who spends time getting to know and building a relationship with patients. If the argument sounds familiar, it is. We are back to a narrow, engineering model of health care which we rejected in the previous chapter. The NHS's new management ideology feeds into the existing prejudices of most doctors and between them reinforces a very particular understanding of health care and a very specific model of what constitutes good treatment.

Cost Cutting

The second important component of the new managerialism has been its legitimation of cost cutting. It is a relatively narrow step to move from ideas of performance to concepts of efficiency and productivity and it would be disingenuous to pretend that performance indicators, as they are currently constituted, do not encourage administrators and doctors to equate good health care, or good medicine, with a good position in the PI league table. Success is judged by whether your PIs are better or worse than your neighbours and there is an enormous temptation for health authorities to seek to raise their activity levels to those of the most productive without any compensating ability to decide whether the result is a healthier or more satisfied population. PIs suggest that the best authorities are the most efficient, and efficiency is measured in terms of maximum measurable output for minimum measurable input.

This natural tendency has been deliberately encouraged by government ministers and the DHSS, who have made it abundantly clear that the primary task of the new management should be to root out inefficiency and cut costs. A widespread conviction among Conservative supporters and back-bench Tory MPs that the public services are wasteful and profligate has been taken up, in the name of general management, by the NHS's new general managers. Good management comes to equal increased performance *and* lower costs.

The Conservative administration of 1979 set the tone when it brought in the vice chairman of Marks and Spencers, Sir Derek Rayner (later Lord Rayner) to conduct a series of investigations into inefficiency in the civil service. The message was clear: civil servants and public administrators could not be trusted to put their own houses in order. What was needed was a professional (private sector) manager to do it. In 1982 this exercise was extended to the NHS.

The early Rayner scrutinies, as they were known, looked at such arcane but safe topics as the collection of payments due to health authorities under the Road Traffic Act and the storage of supplies and catering. Government announcements suggested very substantial savings, running into many millions of pounds, and the House of Commons Public

Accounts Committee welcomed them as showing 'that central initiatives can act as a significant spur in directing the attention of health authorities to particular areas where VFM [value for money] can be achieved'.[18] Savings at a local level have tended to be well below what was expected nationally but, according to the Public Accounts Committee, 'these initiatives can nevertheless make a major contribution to health authorities' cost improvement programmes'.

It would be churlish and naive to deny that there have not been areas of serious inefficiency and wastefulness in the past and that some are still around. But how much room is there for a genuine cost improvement programme and how much importance should be attributed to it? To a large extent the answers have already been decided. For the last three or four years government funding to the Health Service has been predicated on the assumption that good managers will continue to produce substantial savings and that therefore the overall figure for new money to the Health Service can be allowed to fall. Health authorities have been forced to make saving a top priority in order to balance their books and meet new demands for treatment and care. How have they done this? One route has been via an annual series of DHSS-inspired cost improvement programmes.

Cost Improvement Programmes

For several years in the early 1980s the Department of Health imposed blanket efficiency savings on local health authorities, but in 1983 the Department concluded that a pure cash-saving exercise did not give a true indication of increases in efficiency. Many authorities were merely juggling their books or postponing developments until the next financial year. The Department therefore changed tack and in 1984–85 introduced the concept of cost improvement programmes, the difference being that while an efficiency saving is merely a sum of money, a cost improvement programme is intended to force authorities to state not only what they are saving, but how they got there. The exercise was underpinned by the steady growth of PIs which allowed authorities to identify areas where they appeared to be less productive than other districts. No specific national targets have been set, but each district is obliged to include cost improvement measures in the annual planning programmes which go before government ministers and if they are not considered adequate, a district can be told to go back and think again.

The exercise is still in its infancy but the DHSS has made it clear that it expects substantial savings to flow from it. In 1984–85 cost improvements amounted to a startling £105 million, compared with a planned improvement of £107 million, and in 1985–86 the figure rose to over £153 million. In a review of the exercise in 1985 the House of Commons' Public Accounts Committee concluded: 'For both years the target value of cost improvements contained in the individual programmes submitted by different authorities varied significantly, both as between districts and as between regions. It was clear from the reviews undertaken by the DHSS and the National Audit Office that not all sources of cost improvement had been explored by all authorities. Although it is unrealistic to expect all authorities to examine all potential sources of cost improvements simultaneously, it seems likely that larger savings could be achieved if all authorities tackled the search for cost improvement with equal vigour.'[19]

Manpower

One of the more successful areas of saving has been in employment practices. The number of people employed in the NHS is enormously important in determining the cost of the service. Some 70 per cent of its budget goes on wages. It has been a sensitive area ever since finance became a major political issue. But in 1984 the Department of Health decided that something more dramatic than the traditional exhortations to districts to look more closely at their manpower needs was required and it imposed a national manpower target. This required the Health Service to reduce its manpower levels by 0.5 per cent and this figure, slightly modified, has been repeated in later years. The national figure is broken down into regional figures which are then translated into targets for the districts. They in turn are obliged to incorporate them into their annual planning programmes. In 1984 health authorities more than matched the target and NHS manpower fell by more than 4,500. In 1985 there was a further reduction of 3,300. But these savings have not been across the board. Two groups of employees have been particularly squeezed. Since 1982, the peak year for employment in the NHS, the only category of staff to fall significantly has been ancillary workers where there has been a dramatic drop of 25,000 jobs. Much of this has been gained by contracting out the services to private enterprise and some of the savings may be a partial paper exercise; staff are simply transferred from one set of books to another. But, as we will see later, there can be no question that ancillary staff are under enormous pressure. Every other important category of staff has risen, some quite markedly. So-called professional and technical staff have risen by over 20 per cent. This category covers such staff as laboratory technicians, chiropodists, speech therapists and radiographers and reflects the increased importance of high technology in medical care and the growing importance of the rehabilitative and therapeutic professions. Doctors and dentists have increased by 5 per cent and administrative staff by 0.9 per cent. The only other group of any size is nurses, who have increased by about 1 per cent. But this figure hides the fact that their work load has been sharply increased because of the more productive use of hospital beds and the inclusion of some nurses in a managerial rather than nursing function. A 1 per cent increase represents a net reduction in the patient/nurse ratio and nurses certainly feel under considerable strain.

How much longer can the government continue to base its funding on such substantial savings in people and money? At some point, when the more obvious areas of 'inefficiency' have been tackled, a law of diminishing returns will set in. 'It is possible that a continued improvement in activity at the same rate as over the last ten years will not be achieved. The activity improvement record over the last ten years has been helped by some relatively easy gains in regions with a high average length of stay (in hospital), at the beginning of the period,' two commentators wrote in a recent study of Health Service expenditure trends.[20] How far we are from the point of diminishing returns nobody knows.

Meanwhile many district health authorities now regard the cost improvement programme as an essential mechanism for balancing their budgets. It has become a means for making up for shortfalls in government funding without closing down whole departments. The National Association of Health Authorities, an independent research and lobby organisation on behalf of health authorities, conducted a survey in 1985–86 which showed that some 40 per cent of the 148 authorities responding had used cost improvement savings to meet shortfalls in the money allocated to them for new, nationally agreed pay awards. For some authorities it has also become the only mechanism they have for funding new services.[21]

It is easy to forget, in all the jargon, what this means. The triumph of managerialism has been to successfully shift our attention away from a concern with the overall quantity of funds available to the Health Service to a preoccupation with how they can best be used. 'The language of objectives is changing,' as one commentator put it. 'It is becoming that of service outputs. The emphasis is now on increasing not what is being put into the NHS (the 1970s mode when optimism about economic growth had not yet died) but what is coming out of it. There are so many extra births in hospital, so many extra heart operations or hip replacements.[22] In other words, as inputs become static, the focus of attention has shifted from the adequacy of what is going in to how much can be squeezed out. Management holds out the promise that the NHS can still flourish even when its budget is falling.

But the shift in attention is not just from inputs to outputs. Inputs raise questions of need. It is no coincidence that the main formula for determining inputs into the Health Service, the RAWP formula, is premised on an understanding of need. But outputs merely raise questions of efficiency: how productively are health districts using their resources as judged by their comparative PIs? Thus outputs replace inputs and efficiency replaces need.

This is already happening. As the RAWP formula becomes increasingly meaningless in the face of the economic squeeze, measures of efficiency are being used to distribute resources. PIs mean it is possible for a regional health authority to establish a theoretical 'ideal' level of efficiency and then to distribute resources to its districts according to their distance from this target. An approach like this has been adopted by North East Thames regional health authority. The region has created three efficiency bands, and resources are distributed to districts according to where they fit into them. The top one third most efficient districts in the region can expect to receive 99.7 per cent of their previous level of funding, the 0.3 per cent difference being made up from further efficiency savings; the second one third will receive 99.5 per cent of the previous year's funds and the bottom one third will get 99.3 per cent with the expectation that they will have to find 0.7 per cent of their funds from efficiency measures.

This distributive mechanism has not been generally adopted yet, but there have been loud hints from the DHSS for some time that RAWP is slowly on its way out and that some system, based on efficiency, is likely to take its place. The worry must be that in substituting efficiency for need the Health Service is turning in on itself and away from the social context within which it is operating. Output is influenced by the nature or quality of the need it is meeting. There is a difference between meeting the needs of a prosperous, mobile and well-housed professional population and those of an economically and socially depressed inner-city area. But the new managerialism is fostering an inward-looking and self-preoccupied administration which has neither the inclination nor the tools to look beyond its own immediate problems. Means have become ends and the tools of management – performance indicators, reviews, planning and cost improvement programmes – have taken on a life of their own. They have reinforced a narrow, engineering understanding of health and ill health which is divorced from the social context in which it is operating.

Broader issues of how comprehensive the service being provided is – whether it is catering for the full range of health needs, and whether it is available equally to all (issues briefly addressed in the mid-1970s) – are no longer on the agenda.

The new managerial tools have allowed the National Health Service to make very large savings in the name of efficiency and value for money, but we should be aware that they are crude and occasionally misleading instruments and that we may not be able to measure, and therefore may not even be aware of, some of the things we are losing. We cannot be sure that a local hospital which does well in the performance indicator league table is also offering a good service to its local population.

*   *   *

What has the management revolution meant on the ground? In Haringey life revolves around the cost improvement programme. On the basis of the RAWP formula the district is considered to be one of the better funded parts of the country and it is being obliged to live on a falling budget. Its apparent affluence is further emphasised by its PIs which show that it is exceptionally well endowed with hospital beds and doctors compared with many other parts of the country.

But the procedure for applying the RAWP formula to Haringey is, at best, rough and ready and indicative of a general crudeness of approach. It is based on a series of assessments and calculations, some of which we are now familiar with. It begins by deciding the base-line population against which the district's services are to be measured. This is not as simple as it sounds since hospitals, which are the main consumers of resources, do not have formal catchment areas; people are free to go to any hospital they choose, regardless of where they live. The *resident population* living around a hospital is therefore not necessarily the same as the population which uses that hospital and consequently the resident population is only a crude measure of that hospital's *planning population*. To give an illustration, hospitals in London are heavily used by people who live in the surrounding home counties but travel to London to work. This means that the planning population of a hospital in the home counties may well be less than its resident population, while the opposite will be the case for London hospitals.

To calculate a planning population more accurately the DHSS has developed what it calls a 'gravity model' which is based on the assumption that people are attracted by the existence of a service but deterred by the time and difficulty involved in getting to it; the nearest hospital may not be the most convenient. Put simply, the model looks at the demand the surrounding population has historically made on a particular hospital, makes an allowance for any developments at that hospital which may increase or decrease this demand (the opening or closing of a service) and calls this the hospital's planning population. For example, the population of Haringey is around 200,000 people of which, say, 80,000 have historically used the North Middlesex hospital. In addition to this, some residents of neighbouring Enfield also use the North Middlesex. Put these figures together and you get the planning population of the North Middlesex.

It is a rather crude calculation. Apart from the vagaries of individual preferences for hospitals, it assumes that demand equals need and particularly in the case of hospital treatment this may not be true. The way in which need is translated into demand is heavily determined by doctors, GPs in particular. Doctors define what is ill health and therefore what is the need for treatment; this happens at all levels of the Health Service but it is especially true of hospitals where GPs act as gate-keepers to most treatment and so demand is a product of what they consider is the need for it, which may not be the same as the actual level of ill health or what other people might consider to be the need for it. In working class areas where GPs and patients may have a poor relationship the margin for error is known to be considerable. A study in south London, for instance, found a considerable amount of what it called 'unreported illness', some of it serious. Of the first 1,000 cases screened, only 67 were judged completely fit and 500 were referred to their doctor. To this crude planning figure are added the additional crudities introduced by the RAWP formula itself and its attempts to weight population on the basis of health need.

These shortcomings would matter less in a period of growth, but at a time of restraint RAWP rapidly loses touch with reality and the figures it comes up with bear no relationship to what a RAWP-losing authority can live on. On the basis of the formula Haringey should lose £7 million over the next ten years on a budget of £37 million. Everybody accepts that it is madness. The district's former administrator, Barbara Young, was despairingly dismissive of the result. 'I cannot conceive of it being right,' she says. 'If Haringey has got to drop from being a £37 million enterprise to a £30 million operation then we might as well pack up and go home.'

North East Thames regional health authority has conceded the point and, as we have seen, turned to measures of efficiency as a distributive mechanism. Haringey fits into the middle efficiency band, which means that it loses 0.5 per cent, or £250,000 of its income for the next three years, which it will have to make up from efficiency measures.

On top of this the district is also expected to restructure its balance of health care between hospitals and community provision in line with the recommendations of the Priorities document. North East Thames region, in accordance with this shift in priorities, has announced a radical reduction in the size of the patient population at the two large psychiatric hospitals and one large mental handicap hospital which serve Haringey. Health authorities are expected to make up for this by providing new community facilities. Haringey has calculated that this will cost it around £500,000 a year. This sum will also have to be internally generated by restructuring and reshaping the character of the local service.

Finally, the health authority is not expecting the government to fund the full implications of future nationally determined pay awards. The upshot is that the district has calculated that it will need to find annual savings of around £750,000 for the next three years to live within its budget and carry out minimal new projects.

Even these figures could be optimistic. In recent years the DHSS has added AIDS and screening facilities for cervical and breast cancer to the original priorities list. AIDS alone could cost district health authorities thousands of pounds. It has been estimated that the cost of treating the average AIDs victim could be as high as £20,000 per person.[23]

Where will the money come from? Some will come from cost improvement or value for money exercises but the bulk will come from a rationalisation of the district's acute hospitals. In 1983 the new district health authority reaffirmed the pre-1982 administration's hospital rationalisation plan and closed down the Prince. It opted for a two-site district general hospital based at the North Middlesex and St Ann's hospitals. But these two hospitals in turn now face rationalisation.

CHAPTER THREE

A Hospital on Hard Times

At a point roughly one mile east of the big Cambridge
roundabout, where the North Circular Road, curving its way
across the outer suburbs of north London, crosses the A10
London to Cambridge road, there is a newish stretch of dual
carriageway on the North Circular where the traffic tries to
speed up. The road is bounded at this point by a high wall
which picks up the almost constant roar of passing vehicles
and seems to magnify it, bouncing it back across a narrow
strip of pavement and encouraging what pedestrians there
are to hurry on their way. It is a noisy, dusty, inhospitable
spot. Behind the wall and overlooking the road is a large red-
brick building in the Victorian institutional mould, with
symmetrical rows of windows, many of which stare curtain-
less and blank at the passing traffic. It is the first and
probably only glimpse most people get of the North
Middlesex, Haringey's most important hospital.

The upper floors of this building, built in the 1930s to a
1900s design, are virtually derelict, the former residential
quarters of junior medical staff and nurses, now mostly
untidily abandoned or turned into offices. Bits of paper have
been stuffed into gaps in the ill-fitting windows and
ventilators have been papered over to keep out the drafts.
Next to it is a ten-storey, 1970s concrete and glass tower
block, the modern part of the hospital, with maternity,
gynaecology, ophthalmic and some surgical beds, and next
to this a 1960s outpatients department designed in the 1930s

and heavily stamped with the style of that period. Behind and stretching away from the road are the main ward blocks, a jumble of buildings dating from the turn of the century which have served out their useful life. The medical block, built in 1893, stands gauntly in the middle looking from a distance more like a prison block than a hospital. Until fairly recently it had no mains drinking water and patients drank water from a storage tank in the roof. The neighbouring surgical blocks are of a similar period. The overall impression is of a mess; an unloveable study in the down-market architecture of the last hundred years.

The North Middlesex has never been what might be called a popular or well-loved local hospital. Nobody has ever written a loving biography or painted its picture and there is little sense of civic pride or celebration about the place. In the 1930s it was run down by Middlesex County Council which planned to redevelop it but was cut short by the Second World War. It has always suffered from its location, midway between Enfield and Tottenham. Between 1946 and 1974 it was the responsibility of the Enfield hospital management board, but perched on the edge of the poorer end of Enfield, it always took second place in the hearts and minds of local politicians and people to the development of a new central Enfield hospital. In 1974 it passed to Haringey health district, who also regarded it as a marginal hospital on the northern edge of Tottenham and virtually ran it into the ground during the lean years of the 1970s, clocking up the biggest backlog of maintenance in cash terms in the North East Thames region. Like many of London's smaller hospitals it has also lived in the shadow of the big teaching hospitals which for the last forty years have attracted the lion's share of new money, staff and talent. More recently it has found itself in competition for resources with new and expanding hospitals in the commuter belt and home counties around London which are being upgraded to keep pace with the growing 'over-spill' population around them at the expense of London's traditional hospitals.

It is perhaps symbolic of local indifference to the North Middlesex that when the North Circular Road was re-developed in the 1970s it sliced a six-lane carriageway through the hospital's grounds rather than taking a more northerly route through a residential area. Today motorists are said to use it as a short cut to avoid the evening traffic jam at the Cambridge roundabout, heedless of their effect on ambulances or the emergency services.

Despite this history of neglect the area served by the North Middlesex is considered to be overprovided with resources in national terms and the hospital is set to lose still more money in the coming years. Haringey health district, faced with a declining budget, is looking to the hospital, as the major consumer of resources, to provide its biggest proportion of savings; indeed the district's financial strategy is predicated on squeezing savings out of the North Middlesex. There is a conviction among its administration that a history of relatively poor funding is no indicator that a hospital is providing good value for money or that resources are being well used. Some £2 million has already been trimmed from the hospital's budget and the pattern is expected to be maintained over the next few years.

To the casual observer this pressure to find savings can sometimes seem overwhelmingly petty. It is an ordinary morning in a large and cluttered office. The phone rings. A car belonging to one of the district's community midwives has broken down, can she hire a replacement? You can see the administrator's hackles rise as he takes a deep breath before the words come out in an unstoppable torrent: 'No, no and no; there is no money; the transport budget is fully committed; I'm not prepared to authorise any more expenditure; she'll have to go by bus; it's her hard cheese.' You can tell he has said it all before and almost as he puts the phone down it rings again; it is a complaint about dirt on one of the medical wards. The administrator looks grim and promises without great conviction that he will do something about it. You can see that he has said that before too and probably means it each time but there is not a lot he can do. He has had phone calls like this each morning for what feels like a lifetime and there is no reason to expect a let-up.

Outside, waiting at the bus stop, I met a man who told me in tones of incredulity that he had just taken in toilet rolls for his son because the hospital had run out of them. The following day in the outpatients department a woman recounted how she had had to take in salt for her daughter, who had been prescribed salt baths, because the hospital did not have any. Another woman said her son had complained about being given dry toast for breakfast and had been told that the ward only got supplied with butter twice a week and that morning it had run out.

Yet from a managerial point of view the hospital's new, leaner regime has been a triumph. The North Middlesex today is treating more people at a lower cost per patient than at any time in its recently recorded history. On the basis of a number of critical performance indicators the hospital has scrambled its way up from the bottom of the region's efficiency 'league table' to somewhere near the middle. These gains are seen to vastly outweigh any temporary and minor shortages the process of arriving at them may have created. On central issues, the argument goes, the hospital is doing better than it has ever done before.

But, if the district's financial strategy is to remain on course, these figures will have to continue to improve. The authority needs to find further savings of nearly £1 million from a continued rationalisation of its hospital if it is to live within its revenue allocation. This chapter looks at some of the different areas of hospital activity that are expected to contribute towards this figure.

The district health authority has made it clear that a substantial proportion of the cuts will have to come from a further rationalisation of hospital beds. These have already fallen by several hundred in the last five years but another hundred will need to go in the next three years. National performance indicators suggest that the district could also make savings in medical manpower and the so-called hotel services – cooks, cleaners, porters and so on – and a study by the House of Commons National Audit Office argues that, nationally, millions of pounds could be saved by a better use of nurses. Performance indicators further suggest that the regional health authority could prune its budget by a rationalisation of regional medical specialties which in turn would help some districts save money.

But what is all this likely to mean for the hospital service available to local people? What are Haringey's waiting lists and times like and are they likely to grow? Will it mean a fall in standards of patient care and will the quality of the local service suffer? And, finally, what does it mean for the people who work in local hospitals?

Beds

It is 9.45 a.m. on Mark Ward, one of the North Middlesex's four medical wards. Dr Sandy Pringle, a consultant physician, and his firm of three junior doctors – a registrar, a senior houseman and a medical student – are making a ward round. The firm has about a dozen patients on the ward and they seem to make slow progress as, in their white coats, they cluster round a trolley of medical records which they gradually push up the middle of the ward, followed by a ward sister. They talk to patients and they talk to each other. Curtains are drawn around beds and they conduct brief examinations, emerging to consult the records. One man has missed three successive appointments at the local authority assessment centre for the elderly because the ambulance has turned up too late. Another appointment is made. The background chatter is punctuated by shouts from a clearly disturbed man who probably belongs on a psycho-geriatric ward if such a place existed in Haringey. Pringle consoles a man in his thirties who has been paralysed by a stroke and is now a long-term resident of the hospital because there is nowhere else for him to go. It takes about an hour before we cross the hospital site and begin to visit medical patients who cannot be fitted into the overflowing medical wards. On one we meet an elderly man who had waited four hours on a trolley in the casualty department the previous evening because the hospital had temporarily run out of beds. He had ended up on a ward specialising in blood complaints at 12.45 a.m. and was considered lucky. The alternative was a night on the trolley or an ambulance home which would have been difficult in his condition. By the end of the round we have visited medical patients scattered across the entire hospital campus. It is not always as bad as this but during the winter months the medical department is chronically short of beds in its own designated wards, and houses its patients wherever it can find a space. Some of the other clinical departments are in an equally tight position. Against this backdrop, plans to reduce the number of beds at the North Middlesex can seem perverse.

Several years ago, however, Health Service planners put together a model which enabled them to calculate how many beds a hospital 'should' need to serve a given population. The model assumed a certain level of efficiency or productivity per bed and provided national and regional planners with a yardstick against which to measure the performance of any particular health district. A district with more beds than its theoretical ideal, or norm as it came to be called, was clearly operating less efficiently than it might and was a legitimate target for reductions in its budget. When the yardstick was applied to Haringey it was discovered to be well above its bed norm. It was using too many beds to treat too few people. When I met the district's chairman, Lawrence Bains, he told me in no uncertain terms how important he believed it was to change this:

We have in the past kept people in bed very much longer than elsewhere in the Health Service; in some cases two or three times longer. That all takes more beds and what we call hotel services – food, portering, cleaning and all the rest of it – and it clutters up the hospital with people who in other districts would already have been returned home. Now there is a problem of course, it's not quite as simple as that, because it depends on what sort of home you are going to and how well you are going to be looked after and, of course, we understand that. But even equating ourselves with similar low income, inner London areas, we are still, or were, very slow in turning patients over. We are trying to improve that and it will make a tremendous difference to costings.

The bed norm model is based on a version of the 'gravity throughput' model we have already looked at, broken down this time by hospital specialism rather than health district. It showed that Haringey had twice the number of surgical beds it should have had if they were being used as efficiently as possible, nearly one-third too many maternity beds, 50 per cent too many gynaecology beds and nearly twice the number of general medical beds. In all cases one of the reasons for the excess was that patients were staying in hospital for too long. The district health authority's response has been to instigate a major rationalisation. Some of the more important cuts made so far include surgical beds reduced from 200 to 100, maternity reduced from 124 to 75 and gynaecology reduced from 80 to 37. All are now concentrated at the North Middlesex, with the exception of a few non-emergency surgical beds at St Ann's, with the savings coming primarily from the closure of smaller hospitals in the district like the Prince of Wales, the Bearsted maternity hospital and the Wood Green and Southgate cottage hospital. Further reductions, particularly in surgery, are planned for the future. There has had to be a corresponding increase in the speed at which patients pass through them and the district's 75 maternity beds are now handling the same number of births as the previous 124, while the length of stay in the surgical wards has dropped from 8.42 to 5.5 days. The only major specialty which remains to be tackled is general medicine which, with roughly 200 beds – 100 at the North Middlesex and 100 at St Ann's – is considered to be some 80 above the regional norm, while the length of stay in them is reckoned to be about 1.5 to 1.75 days too long. But figures in this case are deceptive. Many medical beds are occupied by patients who should technically be in a geriatric ward, but Haringey does not have enough of them and until it does it is impossible to bring the medical wards more closely into line with what is considered a suitable number for the strictly medical work load.

Even at this mid-way stage there is no question that, regardless of what PIs may say, the slimming-down exercise can sometimes be extremely painful. It has, from time to time, generated enormous pressures on the remaining beds, particularly in the surgical department. The hospital's casualty department, adjoining the North Circular Road and not far from the M11, is reckoned to be one of the busiest in north London and it is not unusual for patients to wait on trolleys in the corridors and ante-rooms for anything up to three or four hours because the hospital has simply run out of spare beds to put them in. On one winter day, while I was researching this book, the casualty department admitted twenty-two patients at a time when there were only eleven spare beds in the hospital. Doctors and nurses were despatched to find people who could be moved early; seven were sent across the district to St Ann's in south Tottenham and another four were sent home early. It was some hours before the blockage could be cleared.

Intense pressure like this from the accident and emergency department has a knock-on effect on routine non-emergency admissions. The partially rationalised surgical beds are easily swamped by a spate of emergency admissions which force emergency patients into beds previously allocated to non-emergency surgical cases. People's operations are then cancelled at very short notice. This, in turn, reverberates throughout the rest of the week or even weeks, pushing back people who have already waited months for an operation. Occasionally a system of what is known as 'double parking' is used to relieve the pressure. A partially recovered patient is moved to a day room while the bed is used to admit a day patient who, it is assumed, will be able to go home by the

evening so that the bed can be returned to its original
occupant. It is not a popular arrangement with staff who
worry that if the day patient does not recover in time they
are faced with accommodating two people in one bed!

Pressure on the medical wards is more seasonal – more
people go down with medical complaints during the winter –
but even in their unrationalised state the wards overflow
during the winter months. Frequently the hospital runs out
of them altogether and as on the surgical wards, emergency
admissions are delayed while existing patients are juggled
around to create space and the occasional non-emergency
admission (medicine does not have many of these) is
cancelled at the last moment. Partially recovered patients
may be moved to a non-medical ward, while others may be
sent home or across the district to St Ann's.

Sandy Pringle described a fairly typical afternoon's outpatients clinic. 'I'm going to see a man now who I have
provisionally booked in and I am pretty sure will need a bed,
but I know that there isn't one so I'll have to arrange for
somebody to go home when he arrives. After that I'm going
to see a woman with very bad circulation problems in her
legs and I'm pretty sure she will need a bed too and I'll have
to do a bit more shuffling around.'

The system works but it is hard to escape the feeling that
the hospital's economies are being purchased at the cost of
patients' time, money and occasionally health. People
classed as non-emergency admissions can be seen waiting in
day rooms for a bed later that day. Some are called in for
pre-operative checks and paper work and then, instead of
being admitted as they used to be, are sent home to await a
free bed a day or so later. Others are sent home early and
expected to return as day patients for post-operative checks.
The effect of last-minute cancellations can be particularly
traumatic. Imagine the plight of Ann Smith, a single mother
who had been expecting to go into hospital for a cervical
cancer check for months. As the admission date approached
she prepared herself for what she knew would be a painful

but necessary investigation and arranged her life and that of her family around it. The children were told and arrangements made for them to stay with a relative; the school was notified of their pending absence; a neighbour was asked to look after the dog; her employer and her work mates were informed. And then unexpectedly there was a phone call from the hospital telling her it was all off and they could not say exactly when it would be on again – tomorrow, the day after, perhaps next week. It felt like the end of the world. Examples like this are not uncommon.

The administration admits the problem but does not accept that the primary cause is too few beds, certainly in the long term. On some days there can be as many as one hundred unoccupied beds in the hospital and there is a belief that if doctors would take the need to improve productivity seriously and modify their habits accordingly, some of the bottlenecks would evaporate overnight. The rest will be taken care of by new developments. The district is building new geriatric wards which will ease pressure on medical wards, removing many elderly people from them. This will leave the way clear to slim down medical provision to nearer the national norm. At the same time the administration is putting its faith in substituting low cost day- and outpatient treatment in the place of resource-hungry inpatient care. This substitution has become possibly the single most important trend in the pattern of national hospital care in recent years. Since 1972 the number of people treated on a day basis has risen from 5 per cent of the inpatient total to 17 per cent, an increase of over half-a-million treatments a year. Haringey is a relative late-comer to this pattern and is anxious to make up lost ground.

Behind this increase in day treatment lies a concept of hospital provision which substantially alters traditional assumptions about how hospitals, particularly acute hospitals, should be used. It proposes that acute hospitals should become centres of short, sharp, medical interventions, with the more prolonged process of convalescence and aftercare taking place elsewhere, usually at home and with the support of an enlarged primary and community medical service. The problem is that the full model, whatever its long-term merit, is not in place today and as a result many people are suffering extreme hardship, above all the old and frail. With the number of acute hospital beds diminishing and too few long-stay geriatric beds, where do they go?

One group who knows better than most the effects of this squeeze are local authority home helps who frequently find themselves picking up the victims of this increased productivity. 'We are constantly having old people who are taken into hospital in the morning and sent home in the afternoon,' I was told by D, a home help organiser for Haringey. 'Sometimes the hospital says it's a social not a medical problem and it's not their business. But the next day the home help goes round and finds the old person on the floor and she'll have to be readmitted to hospital.'

Rifling through the files in the home helps' office, she digs out incident upon incident in the same vein: a woman of eighty-six, admitted after a stroke, discharged the following day, readmitted the day after that following pressure from a GP who said she should never have been sent home; a woman of seventy-five who fell over in the street, taken to the North Middlesex casualty department where she was checked over and asked if she was worried about anything. 'Yes', she replied, whereupon the casualty officer put the fall down to nerves and sent her home. One week later she was found by a neighbour on the parapet outside her sixth floor flat, apparently about to jump. The milkman and caretaker successfully brought her down and back to hospital where, so the story goes, she was checked over, her legs, which had been scratched, dressed, and then packed off home again. 'To me that was a cry for help,' says D, whose staff are the woman's main support system, 'and all they have done is patch her up and send her home. They haven't bothered to find out what the problem is.' Another example is a man of eighty-two with rheumatoid arthritis, a chest infection, leg ulcers and a pulled muscle in his shoulder, who not only cannot look after himself but apparently needs complete bed rest. The problem is that he has just come out of hospital and the North Middlesex cannot find another bed for him.

One home help learnt to be devious in her efforts to keep her elderly 'client' in hospital. She had the only front door key to the woman's flat and took to hiding or disappearing whenever she knew an ambulance was bringing the woman home. The home help knew her client, who was virtually bed-bound, could not look after herself and did not have anyone else to help her. In the past she had been able to bang on the floor whenever she fell over and the neighbour below called an ambulance. But the neighbour had moved.

For many people the hospital system works perfectly satisfactorily. More people are being treated in fewer beds than ever before in the history of the Health Service. If you are an emergency it will pull out the stops and although they may be a bit slow and creaky in parts, they appear to work. People are not dying because of a failure of the emergency services. But what if you are not an emergency? Like a team of jugglers, hospital staff are obliged to deftly shift, swap and catch patients in an attempt to accommodate as many as possible. It does not seem to be a sensible way to run a service and it is not good enough to argue, as some managers do, that today's patients are merely the unlucky victims of a period of change in which one set of services is shrinking before its substitute has been put in place. Should it happen this way?

Hospital Services

The new streamlined model of the hospital has a second prong which is concerned less with beds, as a gross number, than with the range of specialties which they can afford to accommodate. The North Middlesex is a district general hospital. That means it should provide a comprehensive range of medical services to the local population so that nobody has to travel out of the district for anything but the more unusual or specialised treatments. It is part of a network of district general hospitals which cover the country and are designed to provide a comprehensive, *district based*, health service. However, two processes are at work which, individually and together, are gradually reducing the number of specialties and, therefore, comprehensiveness that district hospitals can afford to provide. The first is a national problem and arises from the ever growing sophistication of some of the newer, developing, medical technologies, and the increasing costs and greater capacity of the equipment and back-up teams needed to support them. New developments in brain and heart surgery, radiotherapy, gynaecology and ophthalmology are pushing hitherto relatively traditional areas of medicine beyond the financial reach of the smaller hospital.

Meanwhile as costs go up, money in most parts of the country is coming down and the need to make savings provokes a second form of pressure to rationalise specialties and reap the benefits of economies of scale. Together these pressures are leading to a gradual run-down of the comprehensiveness of all district hospital services and an increase in the number of centralised, regional-wide units catering for people from a wider catchment area. It is a national trend but it is particularly marked in RAWP-losing regions like North East Thames. There is, moreover, an inexorable logic about it which means that once the first specialty is taken out of a district hospital, a spiral of decline sets in which undermines the medical and economic logic of retaining others; to those who have, more is given. It is a logic which is vividly illustrated at the North Middlesex.

In Haringey the decline started with the loss of the somewhat archaic specialty of thoracic surgery several years ago. Thoracic, or chest, surgery has been through dramatic changes in the last ten to fifteen years and in doing so has moved from a relatively low status, low profile area of medicine to a high profile, high status speciality. In the 1950s and 1960s it was primarily concerned with the lungs and the treatment of lung-related illness, not at that period a very thriving or successful area of medicine, but in the 1970s there were important break-throughs in heart surgery and particularly open heart surgery, which not only moved the principal emphasis of the specialty from the lungs to the heart but radically altered the scale and sophistication of the procedures it was called upon to perform. Open heart and coronary artery by-pass surgery requires large and expensive back-up facilities which a hospital like the North Middlesex could never hope to attract and its thoracic unit was obliged to continue to concentrate on the relatively low technology, low status end of the business, while bigger and wealthier hospitals built up staff and reputations as centres of excellence in what became known as cardiothoracic surgery. In the mid-1980s the North East Thames regional health authority established norms for the number of people it believed were needed to support cardiothoracic units and these suggested that on the basis of past demand, a planning population of one million people could be adequately supported by 450 open-heart surgical operations per year. It followed that a region with a capacity to perform a greater number than this was spending an unnecessary amount of resources on the specialty and the region decided it could cut its number of beds. It so happened that three of the four units providing this service were in teaching hospitals and offered the full range of cardiac and thoracic surgery. The odd one out was the North Middlesex and it consequently seemed the obvious choice to go.

But once the hospital had ceased to perform chest surgery, other specialties began to look less viable. 'When they closed cardiothoracic surgery I said at the time that radiotherapy would be the next to come under threat,' recalls George Marsh, a consultant haematologist at the North Middlesex, and medical representative on the district management team for a while, and he was right. A year after the cardiothoracic rationalisation, North East Thames regional health authority employed management consultants to conduct an £80,000-study into the region's radiotherapy services. North East Thames has invested heavily in radiotherapy in the past, despite the uncertainty and even controversy surrounding its effectiveness in treating cancer, but in the face of economic stringency had begun to doubt whether this was money well spent. The study confirmed these doubts. It found that the region provided one of the biggest radiotherapy services in the country, 18 per cent more courses of treatment than anywhere else in the country, distributed across nine separate units – a 'uniquely decentralised pattern of service' – and that it was impossible to justify this because of the 'absence of clear evidence' that it was beneficial and because of the 'high opportunity costs both in capital and revenue' which it entailed. The region decided to reduce the number of treatments by some 2,600 a year, bringing it closer to the national average, and to invest in new, more productive, linear accelerators, which would replace the older and less efficient cobalt megavolt machines and make it possible to perform more treatments at fewer sites. When it came to looking at where these should be, the North Middlesex, once again, stood out uncomfortably. A good deal of radiotherapy is concerned with lungs and chest complaints and a unit which is not supported by cardiothoracic surgeons is less viable than one which is. Two years after thoracic surgery closed at the North Middlesex, radiotherapy went the same way.

There are now worries that other specialties will become ensnared in this logic. George Marsh is suspicious that the hospital's large and well-endowed haematology department could face rationalisation. Some of the department's work has been concerned with the diagnosis and treatment of cancer-related blood diseases, work which is now less viable since the hospital lost its full-time cancer unit. The North Middlesex's medical physics department, which has traditionally been one of the bigger and more successful units of its kind in the region, looks vulnerable. Medical physics provides back-up services for clinical specialties; it handles and maintains instruments and equipment and is responsible for things like the radioactive isotopes used in radiotherapy. The fewer the specialties, the smaller the work load, and so the logic goes on.

Meanwhile, for financial reasons, other specialties are also disappearing even though they are not part of this immediate spiral. Ear, nose and throat, or ENT, inpatient treatment is no longer considered good value for money unless it is practised in twenty- to twenty-five-bed units serving a population of around 300,000 people and in 1985 this ruled out the continued viability of the North Middlesex's tiny five-bed unit. It has been rationalised into the services of the much bigger neighbouring Whittington hospital. The future of the district's infectious disease service is also doubtful. Haringey provides forty infectious-disease beds but demand for them is said to be dropping off, despite biennial whooping cough epidemics, and North East Thames has suggested infectious-disease beds in the region should be halved, with most of them concentrated at Coppetts Wood isolation hospital. Haringey may be left, by way of consolation, with what it describes as a 'residual twelve "isolation type" beds' for low level infections. If this happens the only non-routine specialty left in the district will be ophthalmology. No one can say how long this will be able to withstand the pressures to centralise.

The district health authority has had mixed feelings about this pruning of its services. While it has accepted most of them, it has consistently opposed the closure of radiotherapy on the grounds that it was a purpose-built 1970s unit which provided an excellent service to local people. There is, moreover, a feeling among some administrators that the district is being progressively stripped of its more exciting and potentially prestigious work. One said:

We have recently lost three fairly major services with the loss of ENT, thoracic surgery and radiotherapy. That has an inevitable knock-on effect. It reduces the training opportunities at Haringey's hospitals, the kudos that attaches to specialisms and the better quality of staff that goes with it. What we end up with is the rump, the basic, routine work. Some of us do feel quite strongly about this. We feel that the teaching hospitals win out because they have got the political clout and that the people who lose are the people we serve.

There is more to this than merely professional pique. The irony is that while the rationalisation makes a significant contribution towards the regional health authority's savings programme, it has exacerbated rather than eased Haringey's financial plight. Take the case of thoracic surgery where the region has lopped over £500,000 from the district's budget in recognition of the fact that it no longer has to provide this service. This saving is not returned to the district and therefore, in the first instance, it represents a net loss. It does not make a contribution to Haringey's own cost improvement programme. But more problematically, it is an over-estimate of the real savings the district can expect to make. It may have cost £500,000 to run the thoracic surgery unit, but the district does not save the same sum by closing it, because the building and many of the infrastructural services which sustained it, still have to be paid for. Average and marginal running costs are not the same and the failure to allow for this means that the district loses half-a-million pounds but perhaps only generates some 25 per cent of this in real savings. It therefore not only loses £500,000 but has to find some £375,000 of it from savings elsewhere in the service. Local administrators believe the region pulled a fast one when it negotiated this deal and are determined that similar mistakes will not be made when other specialisms go. Nevertheless they cannot negotiate their way round the fact that the reduction of specialisms saves the region money but does not contribute to the district's own cost improvement programme.

This is doubly irritating because the diminution in

specialisms also appears to have a perceptible, though complicated, impact on the quality of a district's services. Regional health authorities have always argued that concentrating specialties at a few sites *increases* the quality of these services by making it possible to provide the best equipment, the most sophisticated back-up services and the most experienced staff. This may be true as far as it goes, but it is only one measure, or series of measures, of quality. It ignores the quite severe impact on the hospital and health district left behind.

When Haringey provided thoracic surgery the district not only gained from the expertise of that department, but from its influence on others. The X-ray, pathology and anaesthetic departments were geared up to deal with chest surgery and staff in them gained from this experience. Without it they lose both the necessity and opportunity to do this work and there is a net decline in the overall level of expertise in them. The anaesthetic department also lost a senior registrar when thoracic surgery closed because it could no longer offer adequate training facilities; a net loss of a skilled member of the anaesthetic team. More generally as specialisms disappear, there is a narrowing of the opportunity for other medical staff to learn. The thoracic unit held regular seminars which brought together experts from all the surrounding chest clinics and which were open to doctors from other specialisms. It is now less easy for doctors from the North Middlesex to keep abreast of developments in the field. It may also affect the quality of patient services much more directly. Someone with a stab-wound in the chest, brought into the casualty department at the North Middlesex, would, in the past, have been seen by a thoracic surgeon; today they are dealt with by a general surgeon. Nine times out of ten it makes no difference, but on the tenth the extra expertise may pay off.

The reduction in the comprehensiveness of the district hospital service does suggest that whatever may be said to the contrary, national and regional economies are being pursued and purchased at a cost, to not just the quantity but the quality of the district health service in Britain. While specialisms at a regional level may be being improved, there is a risk of a progressive impoverishment in the quality of the district hospital service as the specialisms which attract most kudos are taken away. There is a broader judgement to be made about the justification of bleeding peripheral hospitals to achieve this and whether or not expertise should be concentrated or distributed around a region.

The district hospital service has always been patchy and uneven but in the past, amongst the routine and ordinary, there have been unexpected areas of excellence which have lifted an otherwise unremarkable hospital or service. These are now disappearing and the average district general hospital is a poorer, more humdrum place for it.

Hospital Doctors

George Marsh has watched these developments from his small office at the back of the North Middlesex hospital complex with a growing sense of demoralisation. He travelled widely in his younger days and came to the hospital some years ago in search of a safe job. Friends and colleagues at the time wondered why he was moving to such an unfashionable backwater but it was the first consultant post he had been offered and he was afraid to turn it down. That was fifteen years ago but he vividly remembers his early dismay at the general run-down state of the place, perhaps because it has remained with him ever since. 'It's a dirty, grubby hospital; people don't seem to have any pride or respect for it,' he grumbles in a resigned fashion. 'It's not just the staff, the public don't seem to care either. They just throw their rubbish around as if it was a tip not a hospital.' As he talks bits of waste paper blow about in the car park outside his window. There have been improvements in the last few years, but they are outweighed in his mind by the steady contraction of facilities. 'I don't ever remember the medical profession being so disgruntled,' he remarks, 'everything has become a battle.' He tells the story of the fabled Dixon Wright, a legend among his contemporaries, who treated all around him with swash-buckling arrogance and the hospital department where he was a consultant as his private fiefdom. On one notable Sunday afternoon Dixon Wright phoned his houseman from the south coast and bellowed down the line, 'Clear the operating theatre, I'm bringing up a private patient. I'll be there by midnight.' The houseman acted accordingly; it was more than his life was worth not to, but by midnight no one had shown up; 1 a.m. came and no Dixon Wright and no private patient; 2 a.m. came and went. At 2.30 the houseman gave up and went to bed but an hour later he was woken by a furious Dixon Wright shaking him and shouting, 'What are you doing here, who do you think you are – God Almighty!' to which the houseman replied, with great aplomb for the middle of the night, 'No sir, just his houseman.'

The story is told with obvious irony, but would it be wrong to read into it a small measure of nostalgic regret? It is symbolic of a period of consultant power which today's hospital doctors may not approve of, may not even entirely believe ever existed, but which in an unconscious way reaffirms who they are and where they have come from. In troubled times it does their self-respect no harm to be able to call on a tradition and culture in which doctors were men (always) to be reckoned with and God help the mere mortal who got in their way.

Much is getting in George Marsh's way at the moment. The regional health authority has told him that the department of haematology, which he has built into a large centre, is too big and must be slimmed down; it wants to take away some of his junior staff. He is convinced that the standard of medicine in the department will suffer. But the proposed reduction is part of a much wider reorganisation of medical staffing at the hospital which is likely to leave a number of departments smaller and slimmer.

Medical staffing in the Health Service has always been dominated by a series of structural imbalances which have been mirrored in the range and quality of local services. There is, to begin with, an imbalance in the number of doctors in different parts of the country, with an historic bias in favour of the south and south east which reflects the general bias in health facilities towards these parts of the country. Thus, as a result, the regional average for doctors per head of population in an 'over-provided' region like North East Thames is some 20 per cent above the national average. Some of this apparently generous level is accounted for by the exceptionally large number of teaching hospitals in the region – five medical schools and three former post-graduate teaching hospitals – which perform a national as well as local role. But this is not the case in districts like Haringey which reflect the regional staffing level but do not have a teaching commitment. In the wake of RAWP, national policy now is to reduce the scale of these variations and North East Thames regional health authority has told its districts to make a 5 per cent reduction in medical staffing levels by the mid-1990s. This represents a net loss of twenty-one hospitals doctors in Haringey.

But this reduction is not straightforward. Some staff will go when the services they provide move elsewhere, but for the rest the reduction is influenced by two other imbalances. The better known is that between medical specialties and is a reflection of the differing statuses accorded to different areas of medicine. Predictably, popular specialties cluster at the cure end of the cure/care continuum – specialties like surgery and general medicine – while the less popular ones reflect the general lack of interest in subjects like geriatrics and mental health. This imbalance means that the high number of medical staff per head of population in the North East Thames region has obscured the fact that in specialisms like mental handicap and forensic psychiatry, staff levels are *below* the national average. This is no longer acceptable in the post-Priorities document era and the overall reduction in medical staffing in Haringey hides quite big changes between different areas: general medicine down from seven to five consultants and from six to three registrars; surgery down two doctors, while other specialisms are set to gain; mental handicap up from three to seven consultants, paediatrics and geriatrics up one consultant apiece.

The third imbalance is between consultants and junior medical staff: housemen, registrars and senior registrars, the so-called training grades. The hospital service has always relied on a generous supply of junior hospital doctors who, as we have seen, work long hours covering routine and emergency work. The assumption has always been that they would progress in due course to better paid and more comfortable consultant posts, or failing that, since there have never been enough consultant posts to go round, to a more comfortable job elsewhere; usually in general practice or overseas in the 'colonies'. But these escape routes have dried up; the 'colonies' no longer need or want our doctors and GPs have their own training structure. On top of this, the clampdown on NHS spending has virtually frozen the creation of new consultant posts.

The result is a career 'crisis' in medicine in which a substantial number of fully trained junior staff are unable to move out of the training grades. Some have remained in the hospital service in the hope that vacancies will arise, stretching out their time as senior registrars beyond the training period, working as locum (temporary) consultants or becoming what are known as clinical assistants, a sort of consultant on the cheap. They work in a limbo-land with no security of tenure, often poorly paid for the hours they put in. Others appear to be leaving hospital medicine altogether and training as GPs or moving into grey areas of private practice so that there is a serious shortage of junior hospital doctors in some parts of the country. A survey by the National Association of Health Authorities, an independent research body which lobbies on behalf of health authorities, found that in October 1986 nearly half the authorities in

Britain were experiencing a shortage of junior hospital doctors, sometimes quite severe.[1]

Sixty-eight of the eighty-eight health authorities which replied to the survey were short of juniors in orthopaedics, forty-two were short in anaesthetics and smaller numbers in accident and emergency, ENT, ophthalmology and obstetrics. Some authorities said they had been forced to cancel clinics and operating sessions and even close accident and emergency departments because of the shortage. Most said it was contributing to the size of their waiting lists and many emphasised that it was costing them money in advertising and locums. Three had taken to advertising in EEC countries, without much success. Coventry, for instance, said it had spent £20,000 on seeking locums including placing adverts in Germany and Holland. Many authorities said they were spending 'exorbitant' sums on locums, perhaps ten to fifteen per cent more per doctor than they would in the normal course of events.

There have been a number of attempts to overcome this career crisis in the last twenty years but all, until recently, have foundered on the rocks of consultant hostility. One of the more recent, and controversial, was proposed by the House of Commons Social Services Select Committee, known as the Short Committee after the Labour MP Rene Short who chairs it. The committee looked at medical manpower and training in the early 1980s and produced a report, usually known as the Short report, which recommended the appointment of a large number of new consultants and a reduction in the relative number of junior hospital doctors so that the ratio between the two should be nearer parity. It would change the service from what has been called a 'consultant led' to a 'consultant based' service.[2]

Such a proposal, however, threatens some of the basic privileges which consultants have come to take for granted. To understand this, it is necessary to understand a little about how medical staff are grouped into firms which are formally headed-up by a consultant. They are known collectively after the name of the consultant. Each firm is responsible for a dual work load: routine patient care and on top of this 'on call' emergency duties. The system has worked because juniors have been prepared to work the long hours involved, freeing consultants to keep a supervisory eye on what goes on but normally working a routine nine to five day, safe in the knowledge that the junior members of the team are keeping watch during the late hours of the evening and the small hours of the morning. At worst the consultant might expect an occasional midnight phone call from a harassed junior looking for advice.

The system has allowed consultants considerable freedom of manoeuvre to determine their working patterns and many have used it to take on outside consultancies and private practice. It is this freedom which is profoundly threatened by any proposal which would reduce the quantity of junior staff and thereby force consultants to undertake a greater share of both routine and emergency work.

A recent compromise, thrashed out between the medical profession and the DHSS, appears to avoid these problems and to steer a middle course between junior aspirations and consultant sensitivities, but George Marsh and some of his colleagues at the North Middlesex remain deeply sceptical. They can only see the reduction in junior staff disrupting their traditional working pattern and reducing the general level of medical expertise. 'I believe in a long training period,' argues George Marsh. 'It sorts out the sheep from the goats. If you get one foot on the first rung of the medical ladder it doesn't necessarily give you the right to become a consultant, just as if you become a junior manager in Sainsburys it doesn't follow that you will become a member of the board of directors.' It sounds self-seeking to an outsider, but there is no question that he believes it. But it may never happen. Evidence from around the country suggests that many health authorities are so strapped for cash that, even if they wanted to, they could not afford to substitute cheap junior staff for consultants who cost some three or four times as much but shoulder roughly the same work load.

The government, aware that the junior staffing crisis could become politically embarrassing, has attempted to sweeten the compromise by providing pump-priming finance designed to encourage health authorities to take on new consultants. But it is probably too little to make much difference. A number of reports suggest that medical budgets are so tight that some authorities cannot afford to meet existing commitments, let alone new ones. Sir Geoffrey Slaney, president of the Royal College of Surgeons, told a press conference in 1986 that 'wards are being closed, beds are being closed, surgeons are being told to reduce their operating sessions. Many of us, including myself, have been criticised for doing too much work. That is unbelievable. The prime cause is finance.'[3] Some days later Dr Maurice Burrows, chairman of the British Medical Association's consultants committee, told the Association's annual conference that 'scores of acute hospitals are having to curtail their activities for financial reasons'.[4] If these reports are to be believed, pump-priming money will be merely swallowed up by the existing shortfall in medical budgets and junior staff will be left no better off than they are at the moment. Indeed there are signs that some authorities appear to be cashing in on the falling number of juniors to save money, while freezing new consultant appointments. As a result the consultant/junior ratio is being altered by a simple fall in the overall number of hospital doctors.

Money is dominating the character and quality of local services more explicitly than ever before. In districts where funds are particularly tight, the redistribution of staff between the different specialties has come to depend on freeing money in the 'over-provided' areas before new consultant appointments can be made in the under-provided ones. This means losing staff, although it can be difficult to get rid of consultants against their will, and the redistribution of staff to areas such as the mentally ill and elderly therefore depends on the willingness of consultants in surgery and general medicine to retire – a slow and hesitant business. More generally, money is influencing *how* medicine is practised. This is a difficult and slightly double-edged issue. Consultants, as a whole, make poor objects for compassion. It is difficult to defend their enormously privileged position and it is by no means clear that they are making good use of the money that is available to them.

There is a well-documented tendency for every new procedure to become an instant must, whatever its cost or efficacy. Several years ago it was CAT scanning, a system of producing pictures of the inside of the body which, unlike X-rays, also shows up soft tissue. It has proved invaluable in the dignosis of things like tumours. An article in the *New England Medical Journal* gently mocked what it clearly saw as the grossly extravagant use of an expensive and relatively untried new procedure:

> Granted that this technique can give sensational images and granted that it can, in specific cases, provide vital and perhaps lifesaving information, but its relation to other well-established and less costly neurological procedures is as yet undefined and fundamental questions remain to be answered about the relative cost effectiveness of the new computed tomographic scanners.[5]

This is from an American journal. But a UK commentator has written similarly about the recent increase in pathology tests:

> The increase has been sustained and exponential, doubling every seven years. Throughout this period one has heard from clinicians that this increase cannot go on, but it has. It becomes apparent that laboratory staff not only carry out tests requested, but also invent new ones. Moreover the demand they generate by a day spent inventing a new test magnificently exceeds the demand assuaged by a day spent doing an old one.[6]

The NHS would like to control this innovative and experimental streak. Local managements have invested heavily in computers and information systems which make it possible to break down the costs of every item of activity and chart the costs incurred by a consultant, a medical firm or a department. It would be nice to think that this questioning might provoke consultants to think again about their priorities and how they are spending money. But the Griffiths management style is peculiarly unsuited to the task. It shares too many of the values which have historically fostered the growth in expensive diagnostic and medical practices and has little understanding of, or sympathy for, the broader human and social ramifications of medicine.

As a result, what are getting lost are the small, though still important, things. Haringey has put a limit on CAT scans, although the ceiling is much higher than the scanning budget has ever reached in the past and is unlikely to make much difference in the foreseeable future. Haringey is encouraging consultants to cut the size of their outpatient clinics, for example, by refusing to see patients more than once. The logic is that one consultation is sufficient and after that it is either into hospital or back to the GP. The pressure is subtle and indirect but the clear message is that a doctor with too many returnees is either incompetent, inefficient, or both. Sandy Pringle finds it a deeply disturbing trend. He is a caring and approachable man who likes to think about his patients. The new regime fosters a predisposition among the hospital's doctors to make snap and immediate judgements, discourages them from monitoring the course of a complaint before acting – and some, like diabetes or blood pressure, take time to unfold – and dissuades them from arriving at tentative conclusions which can be subsequently altered. It also denies them the opportunity to learn from mistakes because the chances are that unless they are very major, they will never hear about them. It is a discrete and small change, hardly noticeable, but which, in an important way, sets the tone for the kind of medicine which is acceptable: diagnostic rather than people-based medicine; medicine as engineering.

The medical manpower reductions are also threatening

the future of Haringey's second hospital, St Ann's, in south Tottenham. At the time of the Prince of Wales closure, the district's administration agreed to establish what is known as a two-site district general hospital. The concept of the district general hospital has underpinned hospital planning for some twenty years. The idea is that each district should have one general hospital offering a complete range of routine services to the local population. However, in some districts this is not practical or possible. Haringey is a case in point. The North Middlesex, the natural site for a local district general hospital, is too small at the moment and too far from the main population centres in Tottenham. The administration therefore decided to distribute services between the North Middlesex and St Ann's, with both hospitals providing a mixture of acute and long-stay facilities. But the projected fall in medical staffing is making this plan look increasingly uncertain. A reduction in the number of surgeons, for instance, may mean the end of acute surgery at the hospital, an event which in the past, at other hospitals, has precipitated the withdrawal of all acute specialties from a site. If this does not happen then the overall reduction in junior medical staff in the acute specialties may have the same effect. The reduction may mean that levels of junior staffing at St Ann's fall below the number necessary to allow juniors to work a one-in-three rota and if this happens the hospital will fall into the same trap as that which previously closed the Prince of Wales. It will hit staffing problems in some of the junior grades and be unable to provide sufficient junior support for consultants in all the main range of acute specialties. Either way St Ann's would be obliged to fall back on the long-stay, non-acute, specialties, undermining the whole concept of a two-site district general hospital.

The process of decline has probably already begun. In early 1987, the children's department at St Ann's closed because the authority could not afford to staff two paediatric departments. Services have been centralised at the North Middlesex. Other specialties are expected to follow. It is going to leave a huge hole in south Tottenham for people like Joan and Philip Morgan who have come to depend on St Ann's. They have a four-year-old boy called Joey, a late arrival in their relationship and the apple of their eyes. Two years ago Joey developed a debilitating urinary tract complaint which has required frequent trips to hospital. These started at St Ann's. Philip, recently redundant from the Gestetner factory in Tottenham, would walk round to the hospital with him, and afterwards they would cross the road to the park opposite to kick a ball around. They made light of the visits and turned them into a game. Then St Ann's children's department closed, and transformed Philip and Joey's life. It takes over an hour and two buses to get from south Tottenham to the North Middlesex and by the time Joey arrives he is tired and irritable. So is Philip. It is small comfort to them to know that they may be only the first of many south Tottenham residents who are about to feel, in a very direct and personal way, the impact of the health district's financial plight. We can share George Marsh's dismay without necessarily sharing his reasons for it.

Nursing

At 11.30 a.m. the surgical ward looked quiet enough, but the nurses were scooting round like headless chickens. 'Life's a race, it's quite a battle some of the time,' said Christine Debenham in an unexpected quiet moment. 'If you're lucky the patients make it all worth while at the end of the day. Usually. I get very angry though. You know they have a right to care and you do your utmost to give them the care they need. But it's a race against time.'

Nursing at the North Middlesex has been through some rocky patches in the past. Some believe it is going through another one now. Nurses represent nearly 50 per cent of the total NHS workforce, 34 per cent of the total revenue budget. The sheer size of their numbers has made them a

tempting target for any serious cost cutter and while the
volume of activity on wards has turned sharply upwards, the
rate of increase in the number of nurses has remained
virtually static at around 1 per cent since the early 1980s.
The gains in nursing productivity have come from abandoning
traditional staffing levels. The assumption until recently has
been that the average acute ward needed 13.6 nurses to
provide 24-hour cover. This generally broke down to five on
the 7 a.m. to 4 p.m. early shift, three on the 12.30 – 9 p.m.
late shift and two on nights. The pattern and the hours
varied from hospital to hospital, but the numbers were a
near universal rule of thumb which, although never 'objec-
tively' assessed against the actual work load, seemed to fit
the demands of the nursing work pattern; a relatively
intensive patch in the morning when patients are woken up,
fed, washed and attended to, another burst at lunchtime and
in the early afternoon, tapering off to a quieter period
towards evening.

The rigidity of this pattern has been under fire for some
years from managers anxious to raise productivity and
particularly since 1980 when nursing hours were reduced
from 40 to 37.5 per week and hospitals faced the prospect of
taking on extra staff to make up the difference. One of the
biggest guns ranged against it has been the House of
Commons National Audit Office which in 1985 looked at
value for money in nursing and was scathingly critical of its
routine, dogmatic or unthinking application in all contexts.[7]
In particular it attacked the shift overlap as being unneces-
sarily generous, and the failure of health authorities to tailor
staffing levels to the actual level of work on a ward at any
one time. These two factors alone, it suggested, were costing
somewhere in the range of £2.3 to £2.7 million a year in the
thirteen health authorities it looked at. Overall, it wrote, the
'evidence suggests that with the present nursing complement
there is scope for substantial efficiency savings over the NHS
as a whole which might amount to many millions of pounds.'

In fact most health authorities had already drawn this

conclusion for themselves, and although the National Audit Office study suggests they may not have done much about it, most have, at least in principle, abandoned fixed staffing levels and moved towards an attempt to match numbers and levels of skill to the actual levels of work, so that staffing on a ward might vary from day to day and even from shift to shift. The difficulty has always been that there is no universally agreed formula which tells a manager how to match nurses to patients. There are several methodologies available but no particular one which is said to be unequivocally satisfactory for all situations. Some authorities therefore employ a mixture and others have fallen back on individual, and often entirely intuitive, rules of thumb based on knowing the strengths and weaknesses of the local nursing team and the pattern of work on different wards which has prevailed in the past. The NHS management board, tipped off by the National Audit Office study, has found this an exceptionally distressing compromise. 'Frankly it is impossible to defend the situation,' it has written, 'of some authorities using *no* systematic method of determining nursing staff numbers. This is not to suggest that any methodology necessarily gives the "right" answer to nurse numbers . . . but the use of a systematic approach does provide an opportunity to review and if necessary challenge existing practice – and such regular reviews are essential if the service is to respond adequately to changing patterns of patient care.'[8] It might have added that such regular and systematic reviews also provide managers with the information necessary to make the millions of pounds of savings the National Audit Office has identified.

Haringey health district falls into the category of authorities which do not employ a formula which can be clearly enumerated. It has relied instead on the skills of its senior nursing staff to manipulate staffing on the basis of their personal knowledge of nurses and wards. But perhaps prompted by the NHS management board's disquiet, it is now changing this and is piloting an American-generated study which minutely breaks down nursing activity into small component parts so that it is possible to see who does what, matches this against a series of criteria of 'good' practice and comes up with a figure for the number of nurses needed to handle a particular workload to a particular standard. When completed, it will allow nursing officers to replace their intuition with an 'objective' calculation and the assumption must be that this will increase nursing productivity and, it follows, enable the hospital to reduce the number of nurses it requires.

However, in many parts of the country, and Haringey is one of them, the primary problem is not too many but too few nurses, a situation which renders the productivity exercise interesting in terms of establishing goals, but academic in terms of saving money. Figures from the Royal College of Nursing suggest that most major hospitals in the south east of England face this problem. The College argues that the high cost of living and low rates of pay – a ward sister at the top of her career ladder can expect to earn between £7,500 and £10,000 a year for a 37.5 hour week – has forced many to leave the profession, the region or both. On top of this, the size and scale of hospital rationalisations in the south east, where RAWP has bitten most severely, has seriously dented morale and interest in nursing. There are, moreover, national nursing shortages in some specialties like intensive care, operating theatres and paediatrics, which pinch the south east still further.[9] The shortages are, of course, uneven. While there is a universal problem in London, where the cost of living is highest, some of the city's more prestigious hospitals suffer less than suburban and unknown hospitals like the North Middlesex. In fact the North Middlesex is squeezed by both the teaching hospitals in central London and the expanding 'green field' hospitals in the home counties which offer a more pleasant environ- ment and, because of their growing populations, the possibility of expansion, albeit small, rather than rationalisa- tion. The resulting dearth of interest in a nursing career in

Haringey is reflected in both the shortage of recruits to the North Middlesex nursing school, where places have been known to be under-subscribed by up to 50 per cent, and the difficulty in recruiting and retaining trained staff. The North Middlesex depends on the school for trained recruits, but the wastage rate can be up to 50 per cent and as a consequence the district is continually and acutely short of its own staff nurses. On any one day, up to one in six nurses can be from agencies and occasionally it has been forced to close an entire ward because of a shortage of nurses.

Most people agree that such a high proportion of agency staff is less than ideal. To begin with it costs more – about 10–15 per cent which goes to cover the agency's overheads and profit – and while nursing management tends to scoff at the hostility of staff nurses towards their agency colleagues, in an older hospital like the North Middlesex, where virtually no two wards are the same, temporary staff depend heavily on the permanent members to show them where things are and how things are done. When everybody is under pressure it does not make for a harmonious working relationship. Christine Debenham, who works on a relatively specialised surgical ward, speaks for many when she maintains that agency staff increase her work load:

You don't know them and they don't know you. This is a specialised ward and they may not have done this kind of work before. Quite often they are not as conscientious as they should be and they can be quite frustrating; you feel you need eyes in the back of your head with some of them. You have to check what they have done. They don't report back as much as your own staff would. Communication is not so good and they might not tell you that somebody has a temperature. It can put a lot more stress on you.

The extra workload, real or imagined, leaves many staff nurses at the North Middlesex feeling tired, demoralised and overworked. The hospital's management is not overly sympathetic, and talking to the two sides it is sometimes difficult to digest the fact that you are talking about the same place. Managers accept that there are what they call 'peaks and troughs' in nursing levels and that during the troughs staffing in some areas can fall below the desirable level, usually in those areas where there are national shortages of trained staff. But, the argument goes, the money is there to recruit as many agency nurses as are necessary and the troughs are short and relatively rare.

This is not how it feels to the regular staff. On the day I met the Royal College of Nursing's North Middlesex convenor, he told me the hospital's medical wards could swallow an extra fourteen to fifteen staff and 'not notice the difference', and that during the previous week most wards had been operating with one nurse less than required. 'You can function,' I was told, at this level, 'but if it's a busy day you are only going to do the minimum you should for patients. You don't skimp, you just go at a quicker rate. You work like a loony. You skip tea breaks or only take a couple of minutes instead of the full 30 minutes. You work late. There is no time for the niceties. You keep saying to patients "in a minute, I'll be with you in a minute". You don't stop walking. You manage and that's our problem.' Several weeks earlier Sister Debenham's ward had been down to what she described as 'rock bottom'. 'I was getting myself in a state and getting everybody else in a state. All of us (referring to other sisters on surgical wards) have been through some pretty rough times in the last year. Then you forget about the satisfaction and think to yourself, "why am I here"? I've thought of leaving but it's finding something else.'

Nurses have also been directly affected by the rationalisation of domestic, catering and laundry services and this has added to their sense of demoralisation and of being swamped by changes outside their control. 'It's stupid things like paper towels by the wash basin which the domestic should fill up everyday but which get forgotten,' said one. 'You end up doing it yourself even though it's not your job. I don't blame the cleaners; there's a lot to do for one person. I complained a lot in the past because I think standards have fallen and the domestic services leave a lot to be desired, but I suppose I've more or less given up now.'

The North Middlesex has a permanent and perpetual linen crisis and has done ever since the laundry service was rationalised and moved to neighbouring Enfield. For reasons which nobody can satisfactorily explain, more linen goes to the laundry than ever comes back. In theory patients should have a change of at least one sheet every day and a complete change when they come back from an operation. But it does not happen at the North Middlesex. 'I should get 30 to 40 large sheets a day on a ward this size,' says Sister Debenham. 'I have sometimes had none and quite often I get less than half that. You may have somebody sweating buckets who should get a change, but you can't do your job properly because you haven't got the resources; you haven't got a spare pair of bedsheets.'

It is quite usual for there not even to be enough clean sheets for new incoming patients.

Tomorrow there are eight patients coming into this ward so we have got to make eight beds; sixteen sheets and eight pillow cases. But often I don't get one full-sized bedsheet. We phone the laundry who say it isn't their fault. So we phone the administration where there is somebody who is in charge of this sort of thing and they eventually whistle up the basics. But it's a battle. People are admitted and then they have to wait. You can get eight people sitting at the end of the ward waiting for their beds, and the beds are there, but there aren't any sheets to put on them. The doctors cannot examine the patients and we cannot properly admit them because we don't know which bed they are going to end up in.

The administration says it is actively pursuing the problem.

Perhaps not surprisingly, national opinion surveys show nurses to be a depressed and stressed group of people. A survey by the magazine *Nursing Mirror*, in 1985, found that 75 per cent of those polled claimed to have reported 'dangerously low' staffing levels during the previous year and 40 per cent said they had often reported it.[10] 56 per cent said they 'occasionally felt too tired or stressed to work,' but had carried on anyway, 37 per cent said they 'often' felt too tired and 61 per cent said they occasionally felt 'tearful for no apparent reason'. One told the magazine: 'There have been times when my illness would not have been severe enough to prevent my working had the workload, through lack of staff, not been so heavy.'

These findings were more or less replicated in a second survey later that year, which claimed to be the first ever large-scale investigation into stress among senior nurses and ward sisters.[11] It found that one in six expressed dissatisfaction with their job and often thought of leaving. They listed the heavy workload, inability to meet the standards they expected of themselves and poor staff relations as their main problems. 'Staff felt they had too little time to do what was expected of them and were often overwhelmed by conflicting priorities. Problems with staffing were a source of considerable anxiety,' the survey recorded.

There are interesting and telling parallels between the plight of nurses and that of junior hospital doctors. In both cases, plans to rationalise and plan their working practices have revealed stresses and strains in the Health Service which everybody has known about for decades but has hitherto chosen to ignore. They have now come home to roost and, for the first time, we are becoming aware of the financial cost to the Health Service – as opposed to its employees – of taking these people for granted. The irony of the situation is measured in terms of the extra locum and agency fees the Health Service is having to pay for failing to foster proper career and pay structures in the past. Even if a health authority wanted to spend more now to save in the future, it would not be allowed to, such is the tight financial rein under which health authorities are being kept. The saddest part of this is that at a time of record unemployment, including a small measure of medical unemployment, health authorities cannot afford to provide enough employment to enable them to retain sufficient staff to run the NHS adequately.

The management of the North Middlesex hospital is resigned to not saving money on the nursing budget through any increase in productivity generated by the new flexible rostering, but equally it is unable to buy its way out of a situation which almost everybody accepts is unsatisfactory. It shares this predicament with almost every health authority in the south east of England. While districts like Haringey will continue to look for ways of increasing nursing productivity, the principal resolution of their problem lies with the DHSS and the NHS management board which between them dictate national nursing wage levels.

There would appear to be a mismatch between the areas of nursing which are causing problems and those which are receiving attention. The management effort is going into increasing productivity. This may reduce the need for nurses, but it will never be sufficient to overcome the main problem which is a dire shortage of nurses in the first place. Increased productivity may in fact exacerbate this by further reducing morale and increasing the number of people leaving the profession unless it is offset by an appropriate improvement in wages and general conditions.

Cleaners

For five days Daisy Eyres stood on a picket line outside the gates of the North Middlesex hospital to demonstrate the strength of her opposition to suggestions that her job as a hospital domestic might be reorganised. The following week, however, at the monthly meeting of the district health authority, Haringey overrode its own scepticism, and the opposition of its trade unions, and fell in line with a 'request' from the Department of Health to open up cleaning and domestic services at the North Middlesex to outside commercial contractors. The idea was to see whether private enterprise could do the job more cheaply than the existing NHS staff.

The NHS's so-called 'hotel' services – cooking, cleaning

and laundry – have faced what amounts to a double rationalisation in recent years. The spread of performance indicators has shown that some authorities are running financially tighter 'hotel' operations than others and the general availability of this sort of information has coincided with a government desire, probably politically as much as medically inspired, to cut what it considers to be non-essential NHS staff. Ancillary staff are a prime case and regional and district health authorities have been issued with manpower ceilings which have precipitated significant falls in the number of ancillaries. But what has brought the numbers tumbling down has been the contracting-out exercise.

The Conservative party made it a commitment of its 1982 election campaign to open up the public sector to private enterprise in the name of value for money and, duly elected, it promoted a series of initiatives designed to make this a reality. By far the most important, in terms of effect, for the Health Service, has been the opening up of the hotel services to private enterprise. It has not been an edifying spectacle but it has provided the Health Service with probably its biggest single chunk of savings.

The new policy got off to a slow and surprisingly rocky start. The first moves in the process began in 1983 when the DHSS asked health authorities to draw up specifications for their ancillary services – what needed doing, how often and to what standard – and to put these out to competitive tender. Health authorities proved unexpectedly hesitant to act. There appears to have been genuine and widespread doubt about whether it would be possible to disentangle the costs of ancillary services from the rest of the budget and moreover, whether savings would not be made at the cost of standards. Some government supporters and back-benchers accused authorities of being purposely slow in order to hang on to their empires. This underestimated the very real feelings among administrators and health authority members, across a wide political spectrum, that while there could well be important savings to be made in the running of the ancillary services, it was another matter to bring in private contractors to do the work.

Haringey was one of these authorities. Lawrence Bains, Haringey's chairman, is an active supporter of Mrs Thatcher and the Conservative Party, and the health authority had few doubts that savings could be made. Bains recalls:

When the authority was considering going out to competitive tender a NUPE regional officer came to address a meeting to persuade us not to. He said that the unions had a reorganisation plan which could save something like £800,000 a year on the cleaning and catering services. This was the union rep. appealing to the authority. If they say that, we thought to ourselves, God knows what the real scope is. I think they were frankly overstating the case but there were clearly big savings to be made. When both management and unions tell me that substantial sums of money can be made we have clearly still got a lot to do. I remember thinking that it was no good belly-aching about our RAWP being unfair, which I think it is, if first of all we have not put our own home in order. When we can say, look what we have done, we have helped ourselves, now you have got to help us over the next bit, that's reasonable. I'm pretty strong on self-help.

But the authority remained doubtful about the wisdom and practicality of bringing in private contractors.

It is perhaps a measure of the scale of the doubts across a wide political spectrum that when the DHSS issued details of eight health authorities which, between them, had made millions of pounds' worth of savings from contracting out cleaning services, they were shot down by, predictably, the health service unions and, less predictably, by *The Economist* magazine. *The Economist* pointed out:

Three of the contracts were for newly built hospitals or wings with no existing services; the local health authorities had half-heartedly submitted phoney in-house tenders to themselves, which they then duly rejected. In one further instance the authority did not bother to submit an in-house tender at all; it was short of space and wanted some of its laundry to go to an outside contractor. In a fifth case, one private firm replaced another which was not pulling its weight.[12]

Hardly evidence, the magazine pointed out, 'of cut-throat competition between the public and private sectors'. It suggested that doubts still remained about whether the whole business was really about value for money or merely a political dogma.

Is the government interested only in cutting costs to free money for medical care (as it says) or does it (as the unions say) just want more privatisation? One clause in last September's circular said that tenders must not be used to establish a new base cost for running the in-house service. In other words, authorities must not pass outside tenders to the established workforce with a wink and a suggestion that they might learn from it. But if the NHS is really to be run like any other business, should it not be allowed to behave like one?

Left to themselves it is almost certain that a significant rump of authorities would never have adopted competitive tendering. However, once the government had set the ball rolling it came under intense pressure from a lobby of private contractors, and some of its own supporters, to see the job through, and in September 1983 it 'ordered' health authorities to submit timetables by the following March for putting at least one ancillary service out to tender. In doing so it finally scotched any remnants of belief that the 1982 administrative reorganisation had anything to do with devolving power. While it is arguably acceptable, within a framework of devolved decision-making, to set out overall financial targets for health authorities, it is clearly a complete breach of the principle of devolution if the central authority also dictates, and in great detail in this case, how authorities will live within their targets. It relegates day-to-day decision-making to the clockwork implementation of central directives. But despite, or perhaps because of, what was widely seen as heavy-handed government interference in local affairs, a number of authorities, including Haringey, hesitated, in effect ignoring the timetable instruction. Nobody was outrightly defiant, but many found more or less plausible excuses for delaying. It was only the threat of punitive financial sanctions in March 1984 which finally swung the more recalcitrant authorities behind the government's policy. North East Thames regional health authority was instructed to tell its more dilatory districts that unless they took active steps towards drawing up a timetable, the region would make its own assessment of likely savings and deduct them from the district's annual revenue. Haringey gave way. With the hindsight of a couple of years it is possible to see that the hesitation of some authorities had a sound footing in the reality of ancillary work and was based on more than political prejudice, however much that may also have played a part.

Nationally, a number of the early contracting-out exercises were badly botched and the apparently dramatic savings quickly fell apart to reveal hidden costs and problems which had been overlooked. Possibly the worst example of false economies was at Barking in east London where Crothalls, one of the longer established cleaning contractors, had to tender to retain an existing cleaning contract at Barking hospital and in the face of fierce competition cut its contract price by 40 per cent. The saving was achieved by cutting employees' hours by a similar amount. It provoked an acrimonious and protracted strike among the resident cleaners and although Crothalls brought in strike-breaking labour, a number of well-publicised inspections of the hospital suggested that the new cleaning regime was unworkable. The local community health council toured the building and reported that in the kitchens,

there were accumulations of dirt and grease in the corners of food preparation and cooking areas. Food debris had collected behind and beneath equipment which had not been removed for proper cleaning. A thick layer of grease and dirt under the utensil sink and the presence of dead and decomposing cockroaches indicated the lack of regular and effective cleaning. Several live cockroaches were also seen.

This report was subsequently confirmed by the Barking and Dagenham environmental health inspectorate which found that cleaning standards at the hospital were poor and that the cleaning schedules were 'inadequate'.

In Camberwell, in south London, a private laundry company failed to provide separate facilities for washing infected laundry. In Cheltenham, after the introduction of a private laundry service, only 15 per cent of the washed items met the quality control standards established by the district. *The Sunday Times* reported that staff at High Royds hospital for the mentally ill in Yorkshire found faeces, urine and vomit on toilet floors after the cleaning contract had been won by a private company. In Cambridge nurses are said to have found blood and bones on the floor of an operating room. In East Anglia the Royal College of Nursing claimed that nurses were spending time cleaning up in order to maintain acceptable standards and that although the centres of wards appeared clean, areas around beds and lockers were filthy. Maidstone district health authority sacked the private contractor it had awarded a cleaning contract to, and so the list goes on.

Haringey avoided anything quite as dramatic as this but it nevertheless appears to have misjudged the size of the savings it could expect to extract from the North Middlesex's cleaning bill. Forced into putting cleaning services at the North Middlesex out to competitive tender, it decided to go for the job itself by submitting its own in-house tender. The tender won hands down. On paper it cut the cost of cleaning the hospital by nearly 50 per cent – down from £1.1 million to £600,000 – and was thousands of pounds cheaper than its nearest commercial rival. But within months it had become apparent that staffing levels had been screwed down so severely that the standard of the service was suffering. The unions had conceded a reduction in cleaners from two per ward to one-and-a-half, but the in-house tender stipulated one per ward, reducing the numbers from around two hundred to less than one hundred.

Most of the hospital's original staff found the new regime unmanageable from the start and within weeks there were

wholesale resignations. Many frankly admitted at the inter-
views for the one hundred or so new jobs that they would
not be able to do the job in the time allowed and within
twelve months less than half-a-dozen of the original workforce were left. It was a nasty and unexpected shock for the
hospital's management which had anticipated a large saving
in the first year and instead found itself paying nearly
£250,000 in redundancy and early retirement payments. It
was an equally nasty shock for the staff. Daisy Eyres is one
of the very few originals who still remain. She describes a
typical working day on a twenty-five- to thirty-bed ward
under the new regime:

You go in at 7 a.m. and the first thing you do is lay your breakfast
trolley. Then you take a second trolley out and collect the water
jugs and glasses from the patients, say good morning to them,
wash up, refill the jugs and put them back on the trolley for taking
out later on. That takes until about 7.45 when it's time to go round
with the nurse helping out with breakfast. The pace at this stage is
not too bad. You take your breakfast trolley round and then you
take it back to the kitchen and pick up a tea trolley. You walk
round with this giving out tea, coffee, chocolate or whatever the
patients want. You take this back and refill the tea urn. Then you
take the water jugs and glasses out and on the way back you collect
the breakfast things and wash them up. By about 8.45 you should
have finished washing and tidying away and it is time to go round
cleaning all the toilet and bathroom areas: three toilets and three
sinks in one place; one toilet, bath and sink in another; another
three sinks and another two toilets in other parts of the ward. This
takes until about 9.30 and the day has really got going. For the
next half hour you should have time to mop the main ward floor,
get back to the kitchen and take the tea trolley around again. It
can be a bit of a tight squeeze but 10.30 to 10.45 is our tea-break
and you need as much of it as you can get. After that it's time to
mop the two side ward floors, a small corridor and the sister's
office. That takes to about 11.15, time to lay the lunch trolley with
utensils, salt, pepper and serviettes and take them out to each
patient. This might take half-an-hour depending on how long it has
taken to do the floors. Then at about 11.45 you take the cleaning
trolley round and do the lockers and beds with a bowl and damp
cloth until 12.30 when it's time to go back to the kitchen where the
lunch has arrived in tins from the main kitchens. A nurse takes the

lunch round. You wash up the tins and wipe the trolleys – as many
as ten to fifteen tins – so that they are ready for the porter to take
back at 1 p.m. Then you set up the trolley again and go round to
collect the lunch things and put them in the kitchen sink to soak;
back round with the tea trolley, then back to the kitchen to do the
washing up. The sooner you can get all this done the sooner you
can get off to your own lunch.

Two p.m. and it's back on the ward; get the cleaning trolley with
the long handled mop and go round every bed and do the curtain
rails [round each bed] and the runners under each bed [modern
hospital beds have rails under them to make them easier to move].
You do as many beds as you can until about 2.30 – which could be
about half – when it's time to take the tea trolley round again. At
2.45 you go and hoover the day room, wipe the ledges, tidy up the
papers and magazines and so on. There's about half-an-hour for
this and then you've just got time to tidy up after yourself and
clock off at 3.30.

It's a tight and unremitting schedule for a basic rate of pay of
£75 a week gross.

Haringey's management concedes today, if you do not ask
too publicly, that it misjudged the situation. The mass
exodus of staff left the North Middlesex chronically short-
handed for many months and by general consent the
standards of cleanliness plummeted. It is a moot point
whether they have yet recovered. Cleaning staff maintain
they never will unless the regime is modified. 'All you can do
basically is what I call a top clean,' one explained. 'You
make sure you do the important areas like treatment rooms,
toilets and kitchens every day and then you do as much of
the rest as you can. You go in one bathroom on one day and
do a thorough job and the next day you just wipe it over.
Often the corridors and stairs don't get done at all; there
aren't the staff. Sometimes you can trace a pattern in the
dust on the walls with your finger.' She argues that wards
may look clean, but if you know where to look for the tell-
tale signs – curtain rails around, and runners under, the beds
or behind radiators – they are not. Her judgement is backed
up by others, like a sister on a surgical ward who confessed
her ward was not, in her opinion, 'very clean' and that she

had become resigned to accepting lower standards: 'Yesterday the sun was shining through a window and I could see
dust balls under the beds. It had become so thick it had gone
furry.'

It is difficult to know how much, if this is true, it matters.
On the plus side the simple fact is that the health authority
has saved over half-a-million pounds on the cleaning bill of
one hospital. On the negative side there are several
unquantifiable and probably intangible 'costs' which do not
make for an easy trade-off. Does it matter that ward floors
are not always as clean as they used to be, that sometimes
there is dirt under the beds and that corridors are not
cleaned as often as they used to be? Does it matter that in
the name of saving money each domestic has had her supply
of bleach cut from three or four bottles a week to one, that
toilet rolls are now so tightly controlled that bed-bound
patients are no longer allowed to have one beside their beds,
or that the isolation side-rooms on the medical wards,
reserved for patients who are either particularly vulnerable
to infection or particularly infectious, no longer have a
special mop and bucket reserved for them? Nor do toilets;
there are just interchangeable mop heads. The first we will
know is when the gamble does not pay off and cross-
infection occurs on a significant scale. Even then there will
be extenuating circumstances which make the cause hard to
pin down and a more likely scenario is a thousand small
infections, too trivial to be reported and which go unnoticed
– an accepted hazard of visiting or working in a hospital.
That some of these infections subsequently end up for
treatment in hospital, costing the NHS money, will go
completely unrecorded. So too will the fact that, certainly
for many people, hospitals do not feel like safe places to be
in when they look dirty, especially when standards are lower
than most of us would accept in our own homes. We lose
confidence in them and almost imperceptibly we lose
confidence in the Health Service generally.

Even more intangible are the gains that may have flowed

from a working pattern which allowed domestics to be part of a ward team and to talk and develop relationships with patients. Alison Dunn of the Royal College of Nursing has written about this from a nursing point of view.[13] She points out that 'poorly paid staff with reduced holiday entitlement and perhaps no paid sick leave do not make reliable, sensitive members of the caring team' and that many nurses have commented that they felt domestics were an important part of the ward team. She writes about a sense of regret among nurses at the loss of the old relationship with NHS domestics, often built up over the years. Domestics themselves are aware of a changed relationship to patients. 'You used to be able to clean a patient's locker and stand and have a bit of a laugh with them,' one said. 'It's not the same now because it's always in the back of your mind that if you talk for thirty seconds you're going to fall behind with the work, particularly if you spend thirty seconds with each patient.' It used to be common for domestics to run small errands for patients to the hospital shop to pick up a newspaper or card, or interrupt their work to fetch a glass of water. No longer. Yet many domestics believe they were an important source of support and friendship to patients. 'The first person the patient sees in the morning is the domestic. They talk to domestics far more quickly and easily than they will with nurses who are a bit off-putting in their uniforms. They feel more on the same level with us. I think patients liked that and they must be missing it.' Nobody knows at the moment whether this is true and even less whether it matters. Managers today tend to regard domestics simply as cleaners and explicitly not part of the 'ward team'.

What we do know is that the principal losers in this rationalisation have been the ancillary staff themselves. Some 25,000 full-time ancillary jobs have been lost in the NHS since 1982, an underestimate of the real number of people affected since many ancillary staff work part time. Moreover, a major proportion of the remaining savings have come directly out of the pockets of what are indisputably some of the worst paid workers in the country. In a Birmingham health district domestics have had their wages cut by £20 a week and on the Wirral, in Cheshire, by £30 a week, a reduction of nearly 50 per cent. Surely no government can have set out with the intention of robbing some of the lowest paid people in the country to pay for the rest of us to continue to enjoy a health service, yet that is what it has come down to.

The scale of some of these excesses has inevitably increased and reinforced doubts about the validity of the whole programme, at least as it is presently constituted, and contracting out services faces an uncertain future. The number of contracts going to private enterprise is gradually dropping back from the record numbers of 1985 and the private sector has all but admitted that under the present rules it cannot successfully compete with NHS in-house tenders. The private sector lobby would like to see the rules changed so that health authorities are obliged to put hotel services out to private contractors. But much depends on the political complexion of future governments. Ancillary services will never return to their pre-Griffiths state but whether the exercise continues to replicate the excesses of the early days of change or whether it shakes down into something more stable and even-handed, with some respect for the people who staff it, remains to be seen.

Making an Assessment

So is the hospital service doing better than it ever has done before? As always it depends what you put into the calculation. On the basis of performance indicators and value for money, the North Middlesex is a 'better' hospital than it was five years ago. But if we take this further, there are a number of elements which need to go into the calculation before a balanced assessment can be made. We know that the role and nature of the hospital service is changing and that this, certainly temporarily, is causing serious pain and discomfort to some people. We can legitimately suspect that the reduction in the range of local specialties is pushing down the overall quality of the service and that the centralisation of some specialties outside the district has diminished the adequacy of the local service to local people. Neither we nor the health district know the truth about the latter point because although there has been talk of studying the impact on patients of centralising services outside the district, these studies have never been done. We know that restrictions on medical budgets are reducing medical activity in some parts of the country and that the rationalisation of medical staff could involve Haringey in a further rationalisation of its hospitals. We know that the work load of nurses has gone up and that this may be having a knock-on effect on the quality of patient care. We know that standards of hygiene and cleanliness in many hospitals have fallen and that this is likely to increase, however marginally, the risk of cross-infection and decrease patients' confidence in the hospital. Finally, we know that many NHS staff have been traumatically affected by the changes of recent years and we can suspect that their demoralisation will spill over into their attitude towards patients. Some of all this may be reflected in the fact that the number of complaints about the Health Service has gone up in the last year or two and that according to the local community health council the main growth area has been in complaints about the attitudes of doctors and nurses, two groups whose morale has taken a knock.

Anecdotal evidence suggests that in some departments, greater productivity has brought patient confidence tumbling down. The maternity department at the North Middlesex has never had a very high reputation but in the last couple of years it has nearly doubled the speed at which it is handling pregnant women and in doing so, possibly halved their sense of satisfaction. 'They're butchers up there,' I was told by Agnes, who I met accidentally in a corridor outside the maternity department. 'My daughter has just had twins and she was supposed to have an epidural but she's been screaming the place down and all they could say was that it didn't work. There's another mother in there who was also supposed to have an epidural and she's been screaming the place down too. I've been comforting her mother; one grandmother comforting another.' It is difficult to know what weight to give to anecdotes but they reoccurred with an unexpected frequency and I had not gone looking for them. I was told stories of minor incompetences suggestive of staff who are in too much of a hurry, like the story recounted by a home help whose colleague had just had a baby in the North Middlesex: 'I don't know how they did it but when they cut the baby's cord they slashed the mother's leg as well and she had to have six stitches in it.'

In a sense it does not matter whether these stories are right or wrong; they are what people believe the department is like. How do we weigh this against the improvements in performance indicators? One traditional method of assessing the performance of the Health Service is by looking at waiting lists and nationally these continue to rise despite a government-inspired drive to improve them. Waiting lists are subject to all kinds of caveats. Firstly, they can overstate the position because they include people who, for one reason or another, no longer need treatment: they have died; their problem has cured itself or they have gone elsewhere. The last cull of waiting lists in 1984 of people no longer needing treatment reduced the national figure by 40,000. Secondly, they tell us nothing about how long people are waiting for – a much more relevant statistic. Thirdly, it is not clear what waiting lists are actually measuring: they might be telling us that there are too few resources or that these resources are being badly used.

A national survey in 1985–86 of waiting lists for inpatient treatment suggested that Haringey was among the better health districts in the country.[14] On a national comparison relatively few people waited for longer than a year for non-emergency treatment. The district's administration have, on occasions, used this to legitimate the continued squeeze on hospital beds at the North Middlesex. But is this a fair conclusion? What it gives us is Haringey's relative performance. What about the people who *do* have to wait longer than a year? In 1985–86 nearly a hundred local people had to wait twelve months or more for an operation with the longest wait in orthopaedics and ophthalmology. Relatively low waiting lists also tell us that Haringey is using the totality of its hospital facilities – beds, theatres, etc – relatively efficiently, but it does not tell us whether all these facilities are being used equally efficiently or whether some are compensating for others, and above all it does not say anything about the quality or adequacy of the services being provided. It is quite possible for patient throughput to go up and patient health to come down.

A survey in the same year, of waiting times for outpatient appointments, shows that in some specialties the district is significantly below the national average.[15] Across the country it showed that waiting times to see consultants in six key specialties had grown in the last year. The minimum wait for a general medical appointment had increased from 3.4 weeks to 3.7, in surgery from 7.0 to 7.9; in gynaecology from a minimum of 8.1 to 19.0, in ophthalmology from 11.6 to 15.1 and in orthopaedics from 28 to 31.7 weeks. The North Middlesex's position was better in some and worse in others. Medical waiting time, at 7.5 weeks, was twice the national average; surgical waiting times were 6.75 weeks, better than the national average, though varicous vein surgery was very much longer, at anything from 8 to 120 weeks depending on the surgeon. Gynaecology at the North Middlesex was 21 weeks, worse than the national average; eyes were 16.27 weeks, also worse than the national average. Orthopaedic surgery, at 16.3 weeks, is considerably better than the national average at the Prince of Wales (outpatients clinic) but at the North Middlesex, which does not do much orthopaedic work, the list is so long it has closed.

What figures like this really tell us is that whatever Haringey's relative position, the real problem is absolute levels of resources. The question is whether or not it is acceptable that one hundred people are waiting longer than a year for an operation which, although it may not be urgent, is nevertheless necessary and whether or not it is right that a woman should have to wait three months for a gynaecology outpatients appointment to discover whether or not she may have cervical cancer.

Late in 1986, in preparation for a forthcoming general election, the Conservative government asked health authorities to give priority to reducing waiting lists, presumably because of their potential for political embarrassment. But despite efforts to do this, waiting times for urgent inpatient treatment in RAWP-losing parts of the country have increased in the last year, up 20 per cent in North East Thames region and 21 per cent in North West Thames. The most plausible explanation is a shortage of resources. As one administrator explained, 'While you can use resources more efficiently, in the end the more patients you put through the same beds in less time, the more it costs. Hospital costs are bound to rise. Unless extra money is provided you then have to decide from which service or planned development you will take that money.'[16] In the Thames regions there may not be the flexibility to do this and something suffers.

Two remaining points need to be made. The first is that the speed and abruptness of the changes at hospitals like the North Middlesex have pushed patient services to the brink of the safe limits and sometimes beyond them. As one London administrator in a district very similar to Haringey remarked in a memorable phrase: 'If you've got to lose a stone in weight and you've got a year to do it, you can plan a sensible all-round reduction. If you have got to lose a stone and you have only got a week to do it, the only way is chop off a limb.' The seriousness of the situation in some clinical departments, and particularly the pressure on beds, raises questions about the wisdom of a government policy which has obliged health authorities in RAWP-losing districts to move with such haste, often closing facilities well in advance of their replacements coming on stream. We have seen a number of instances of this in the North Middlesex, particularly the rationalisation of beds before alternative arrangements can be made for elderly people.

The second point is that while money may appear to be the main issue in an area like Haringey, it can obscure the fact that in the name of 'value for money' more fundamental changes are taking place in the hospital service across the country as a whole. The new business-orientated management style has brought a new confidence and determination to hospital managers, and new tools with which to push this determination home. But it is not a neutral tool; it contains values and assumptions and is narrowing the scope and scale of the hospital service. It is pushing hospital work towards the curative end of health care where 'cases' can be totted up in columns, leaving the equally important but less tangible element of caring to others. This shift in the role of hospitals and the accompanying impoverishment of the range of services they provide, has enormous repercussions for the rest of the National Health Service. It is to some of these other parts that we now turn.

CHAPTER FOUR

GPs and the Inverse Care Law

The quality of the primary health care service – so-called because it is the first port of call for most people – has never been more important than it is today. The entire rationalisation of the hospital service is premised on the assumption that the non-hospital services will make up the difference. This chapter looks at how GPs, and the community medical service generally, is responding to this challenge.

Dr Nurjahan Karmali is a far cry from the traditional image of a family doctor. As she sits in her temporary surgery in a bright yellow Portacabin in the car park of the local fire station she looks to the future with thinly disguised dread. Outside, a train rumbles by on the embankment which rises steeply beside her window and a heavy lorry revs its engine as it changes gear to negotiate the sharp corner in front of the building. Inside it is dark and cramped. This morning nobody has bothered to take the shutters off the windows and the only natural light seeps in through the half-open door and casts a pale illumination across the waiting area. The whole surgery is not much bigger than a caravan. When it is noisy outside it is difficult to talk inside, but when it is quiet outside voices travel easily through the matchbox-thin partition which separates the tiny consulting room at one end of the cabin from the waiting room and reception desk which fill the rest. It comes as a bit of a shock to realise that this is a National Health surgery in the mid-1980s.

Dr Karmali used to have a permanent surgery a mile or so

away on Tottenham High Road, but two years ago it was destroyed by a fire, later traced to a pile of sheets in the cellar which had been deliberately doused with paraffin. The police put it down to vandalism, just one of a series of random attacks and violent incidents which have gradually worsened over the years and which have left Dr Karmali so shaken and visibly exhausted that each new one becomes a major assault on her emotional well-being.

The surgery had been the target of almost weekly acts of vandalism for as long as she can remember and in an urgent half whisper she says she has forgotten the number of times the front door has been broken down or the building broken into. 'So many times I've lost track. It seems as though we were always having new locks and new doors put on.' The atmosphere of menace and violence carries over into the surgeries. 'They can be so hard. People are under such pressure,' she admits. 'It's difficult to get a thankyou from anybody; they are so rude that sometimes you feel like packing up. They want this or they want that and if you don't give it to them *immediately* you are a no good so and so. People don't regard us as human beings; we are expected to sit here and take it as if we were super-human.'

She tells the story of a young woman who came to see her complaining of an allergic rash. Nurjahan Karmali examined her but could not find anything, so suggested she come back in a few days if it was still worrying her. The woman refused saying, 'I want to see a specialist at the hospital.' When Dr Karmali explained that there was nothing to see and that it would be a waste of time, the woman insisted, 'I want to see a specialist.' The argument became acrimonious and the woman left without an appointment, but that evening an abusive husband phoned the surgery: why had his wife been ill-treated and ignored? Why couldn't she have an appointment? Who pays for the Health Service anyway? He rang off warning Dr Karmali that she had not heard the last of the matter and sure enough, two days later he came back with his wife and, for good measure, his brother and brother-in-law who all insisted on crowding into the small consulting room and refused to leave until an outpatient's appointment was made. With a queue building up behind them and the morning surgery on the brink of chaos, Karmali capitulated with profound misgivings. It was not the first time she had been brow-beaten into making a hospital appointment against her better judgement. She worries that consultants at the North Middlesex hospital will come to regard her as lazy, incompetent or both and is concerned about what this will do for her relations with the hospital and her colleagues – she might become a laughing stock. Nurjahan Karmali's relations with her patients are already so bruised that the rejection of her medical judgement and expertise by one of them passes her by completely, but she clings to her colleagues and their support.

As she talks the stories tumble out in a halting, apparently painful, stream. On the first day in her Portacabin a man pulled a two-foot machette from under his jacket and announced he was going to kill her. She talked him down and he was committed to a psychiatric hospital but for months, each time he was released, the pattern reoccurred and he returned to haunt her. It encouraged Karmali to take a course of action she had been contemplating for some time and give up night visits to patients in case she was assaulted. She is frankly terrified that one dark night she will meet her would-be assailant again and not survive the encounter.

Meanwhile, her anticipated three months in the Porta- cabin have stretched to two years and there is no end in sight. The rehabilitation of her original premises is bogged down in a legal wrangle over who should pay; she cannot find alternative premises in the immediate neighbourhood at a realistic price and she does not want to extend the area of search for fear of losing patients. The numbers on her list have already dropped since she moved to the Portacabin, which has cut into her income, and she does not want to lose more by moving further from her original site. But the choice may be taken out of her hands. The fire brigade wants its car park back and the family practitioner committee, which oversees GP services, may decide she has been long enough in temporary and totally unsuitable premises and can insist that she finds something more permanent and appropriate, but the uncertainty preys on her mind.

Several hundred yards along the High Street, past a hairdresser, launderette, post office and off-licence, is the practice of Dr Harry Isenburg and his partners. Exactly one week after the Karmali fire his surgery, in one of Tottenham's fine but rare eighteenth century buildings, went the same way. Harry Isenburg had been at home with his family celebrating his sixty-ninth birthday at the time. 'It was a lovely birthday present,' he recalls with an attempt at humour he obviously does not feel. 'The fire engines were pumping water . . . the CID were tearing in and out with their flashing lights. It was a nightmare.' But he has been luckier than Dr Karmali. His sojourn in a Portacabin was relatively short and his surgery has been rebuilt and extensively modernised in the process. Harry Isenburg is also, by and large, popular and respected by his patients. He is white and male and looks and acts like everybody's idea of a family doctor and, perhaps because of this, he has avoided the extremes of abuse suffered by his Asian colleague. He has, nevertheless, been profoundly shaken by what he perceives as the growing violence and menace of the neighbourhood. His name plate has been torn down twice, his surgery broken into more than once and now the fire. He cannot help comparing it with what in his mind is a golden age in Tottenham twenty or thirty years ago when there was a strong sense of community and nobody locked their back door at night. As he reflects on it he finds himself impatient and out of sympathy with the changes that have taken place around him.

Like many long-term residents he is, in particular, overwhelmed by changes in the racial composition of the area. His patients have changed from 90 per cent white to 90 per cent black and his understanding and interpretation of what is happening to the area will appear to many people to verge on the racist. Dr Isenburg is Jewish and will find this description deeply offensive but there is no other term for an account of Tottenham's ills which is almost exclusively couched in terms of racial stereotypes. He talks vaguely about social mores and West Indian child-rearing practices as if they were responsible for the changes he sees around him and appears to be almost unaware of the strains of inner-city life as they affect all races. Both he and his wife vividly recall the poverty and deprivation of a pre-welfare state society and cannot understand how people can consider themselves hard up today. He is aware that many of his patients are unemployed but not that they are under any great financial strain. 'I sometimes ask somebody whether they are coping financially and they usually answer something like "well, doctor, not any worse than anybody else," ' he says as if in proof that most people are stoically pulling through. He no longer lives in Tottenham and has cut his hours of work to twenty a week; his knowledge of the area is largely second hand. But this did not stop him regaling me with second-hand accounts of muggings in the street and violence in the schools which reinforce his impressions and fears.

Dr Harry Wallace is a younger and still energetic man who superficially bears no relation to Karmali and Isenburg. But he shares their remoteness and lack of sympathy with Tottenham's population and he wants to leave. 'I was happier in general practice twenty years ago than I am now,' he claims. 'I suppose I'm slightly disillusioned with the attitudes of people. Some people demand a lot and some people are terribly rude and aggressive right from the start. There is no way you can relate to them. Tottenham is a much less pleasant area to work in than when I came here.'

He is critical to the point of contempt of many of the people he comes into contact with, particularly young people:

In this area the socio-economic groups are four and five; quite a lot of five . . . occasionally six (this accompanied by laughter). But most of them cannot help it because they haven't any knowledge and in their upbringing they weren't taught very much and I'm afraid the young school leavers are worse than anybody else because they are so ignorant. There's an Irish expression: they've got about as much sense as a donkey's hind leg. They really are epsilon grade two, you know, they really are gamma minuses. Some of them are quite hopeless and they are going to make hopeless adults and worse parents.

One of the thorns in his side is the now notorious Broadwater Farm, scene of rioting in 1985. It is a high density 1970s council estate of tower blocks linked by low rise blocks and galleries and semi-underground car parks. By common consent it was one of Tottenham's 'bad' estates even before the riots, though how bad depends on where you look at it from. Harry Wallace looks at it from the outside and considers it very bad:

There are certain almost no-go areas around here and the Broadwater Farm estate is one of them. It's not an area I find very pretty. I drove in there one Saturday morning to do a visit and fortunately I had a hard-topped car because a telephone directory came down on the roof of the car from one of the galleries. I'm very careful when I go there now. It's not a good place to go at night; there are a lot of youngsters; robberies, bag-snatching, everything goes on there. I tend not to go at night. I have been once or twice on a summer evening but with great caution.

He has told his partners he wants to retire early before he becomes further embittered and ground down. There are other reasons, like the government's imposition of a limited range of drugs which GPs can prescribe and what he believes is a general move to push GPs towards health centres and salaried employment and away from their present self-employed status. 'I'm not happy with this drug list. I'm not happy with the way they (the government) mess about with us. I don't want to be involved with further attacks on the profession which are going to take place. The writing is definitely on the wall.' But there is a sense that if he enjoyed his patients, other changes would seem less threatening. As it is, they are the last straw. He has had enough of what he experiences as the rudeness, aggression and ungratefulness of the people who pass through his consulting room and, like other doctors in his position, he wants out.

The odd thing is that people in Tottenham make a not dissimilar series of complaints about their GPs. There are doctors known to the community health council as shouters, who verbally abuse their patients; those who are known to be reluctant to make home visits; those who will only provide medical letters in support of social security or DHSS grants under extreme duress and those who have even been known to fail to turn up for their surgery. Both the community health council and the family practitioner committee report that they receive a disproportionate number of complaints from patients in Tottenham compared with the rest of Haringey and that many appear to boil down to a mistrust or poor understanding between patients and doctors. One complaint may be particularly illuminating. Haringey community health council receives a regular stream of complaints about the difficulty of getting onto a doctor's list, especially in the Tottenham and south Haringey areas. It has always maintained that this indicates that there are too few doctors in these areas, which may be true, but there is a second interpretation. According to the family practitioner committee, people moving into Haringey usually experience no problem in getting onto a doctor's list, provided they know how to find one in the first place. The difficulty arises when a patient leaves one doctor and attempts to move to another in the same area. This is much more difficult. GPs, it is said, look with great suspicion on what they regard as 'shopping around'. It smacks to them of 'trouble makers' or a 'difficult' person: 'I think you will find that people who keep chopping and changing doctors tend to get themselves a bad name,' I was told by the family practitioner committee administrator. But if chopping and changing is an indicator of a poor patient/doctor relationship and complaints about problems of getting onto a doctor's list are primarily about people moving from doctor to doctor in search of a better one, then the frequency of this kind of complaint is likely to provide a crude indicator of the quality of the relationship between the two in an area, and a relatively high level of complaints suggests a generally poor level of relationship. This would tally with what we know about a multiracial area like Tottenham where not only do class differences get in the way, but white doctors like Isenburg have difficulty building a relationship of trust and understanding with black patients and white patients may experience a similar difficulty with black doctors. There have been a number of complaints about the Karmali practice, but what remains unknown is how much these are to do with the fact that Dr Karmali does not fit the stereotype of what a family doctor should look and act like and is consequently somehow a lesser doctor. How much was the insistence of the woman with an allergic rash on seeing a hospital doctor tied up with her feelings that what she wanted was a 'real' doctor? How many minor irritants become major irritations when there is no trust, and confidence and communication is poor?

Patients and doctors in an area like Tottenham meet, it would seem, across a frequently uncomprehending and sometimes tense and hostile divide which leaves both sides uncomfortable and dissatisfied, each claiming to be the injured party and each blaming the other for it. Doctors view patients with suspicion and the area with distaste; patients see doctors as remote and uninterested in them and their problems. There is a clash of cultures, outlooks and expectations which leaves little opportunity for mutual understanding of the pressures each is living under and in failing to understand each other they become part of the other's problem; doctors feel under pressure from patients and patients believe they have to fight to get any attention at all. It is a self-destructive cycle which inevitably rebounds on the quality of the services available in the area.

Doctors vote with their feet and an area like Tottenham has fewer doctors per head of population than the more comfortable areas like Highgate and Muswell Hill. Patient/doctor numbers, however, need to be treated with some caution. The figures show that there are 2,358 patients per doctor in east Haringey, broadly the Tottenham area, compared with 2,003 per doctor in the rest of the district. But there is very little guidance on what the 'right' number is. North East Thames regional health authority has suggested an average list size no greater than 2,000 and the British Medical Association has gone even lower to 1,700, but a Royal Commission which looked at the NHS in the 1970s pointed out that there is 'very little known' which would help determine an optimum number, and it recommended that 'considerable research on this important question should be undertaken'.[1] Nearly a decade later this recommendation has never been taken up.

A complicating factor is that the figures give no indication of such things as the hours a doctor works or the range of services offered. A single-handed part-time practice offering the minimum level of service therefore shows up as the same as a doctor in a fully equipped health centre providing a comprehensive range of services. This renders the numbers themselves virtually meaningless. But studies from elsewhere have suggested that doctors in inner-city areas like Tottenham tend, on the average, to provide a poorer and more limited service than in the country as a whole.[2] They tend to be older, to work part-time more frequently, to operate from small or single-handed practices and to provide a minimal range of services. Anecdotal evidence suggests this pattern is born out in Haringey: one in three of Tottenham's doctors is over sixty, compared with one in seven in the better provided parts of the district, and they are more likely to work from smaller practices and offer a more limited range of services. They tend not to employ other staff or to work with other primary care workers like district nurses and health visitors; they are more likely to use a deputising service to provide out-of-hours cover and they have habitually looked to the district's hospital outpatient departments to perform routine tasks like putting in and taking out stitches, changing dressings and giving injections. It is a crude but not seriously misleading generalisation to suggest that the senior partners in many of Tottenham's practices fall into one of two categories. The first is white, nearing retirement — nearer eighty than seventy was how it was put to me — generally out of sympathy with the area and looking forward to leaving. They are men (overwhelmingly) like Isenburg and Wallace who set up in practice when Tottenham was a different place and are now so disillusioned and isolated from the area that their outlook is heavily influenced by their desire to get out. The second category is black, usually Asian, doctors who came to Tottenham in the 1950s, 1960s and early 1970s when it was relatively cheap and there were practices available and who now, like Karmali, feel themselves under sometimes unendurable emotional, social and physical pressure from their patients and the neighbourhood. Both are in Tottenham now through force of circumstance and neither is in a state of mind to think positively or creatively about the neighbourhood or its health needs. At the bottom of their hearts, fighting with the idealism which possibly took them into medicine in the first place, is a growing lack of interest in their patients and their well-being. New, younger doctors occasionally move in, but most can only do so by joining an existing practice where the tone and terms of reference have already been established by this older, controlling group. It effectively blocks the possibility of significant change.

The result is a well-documented impoverishment of the relationship between doctors and patients which strikes at the heart of good primary care. In the early 1980s a DHSS-commissioned study on standards of health in the country reported several studies which suggest that middle-class patients enjoy a better relationship with their doctor than their working-class counterparts; they tend to have longer consultations and to discuss more problems during this period. One study, for instance, found that middle-class patients were able to make better use of a consultation, judged in terms of the number of items of information communicated and the number of questions asked. Moreover, even though working-class patients tend to have been with the same practice for longer (which suggests that they do not all chop and change) doctors seemed to have more knowledge of the personal and domestic circumstances of their middle-class patients.[3]

It is not just a matter of information. The quality of the relationship between patient and doctor determines the quality of much primary care. Medicine at this level is about communication and building a relationship of trust and confidence. Many people visit a GP to talk about themselves and their worries and they may need to learn about their bodies and how they work. They may go with one complaint when the real concern is with another that they are scared or reluctant to face up to and it is at least as important to be a good listener as it is to be a good diagnostician. All this is doubly true when it comes to preventive or forward-looking health care. A consultation period is an opportunity to get to know a patient's habits and characteristics which may have a bearing on future health problems; do they smoke, how much exercise do they take or is there a family history of a particular complaint? It is only when a doctor is aware of these risks that it is possible to plan preventive action. When the relationship between the two is poor, there is very little opportunity or likelihood that any of this will emerge.

The irony is that a working-class area like Tottenham is generally considered to have greater levels of 'ill health' or health need than a district like Highgate or Muswell Hill measured on the usual health indicators. Nearly twenty years ago a South Wales GP called J. Tudor Hart noticed this mismatch between need and provision and propounded his Inverse Care Law. It states that 'in areas with most sickness and death, general practitioners have more work, larger lists . . . and inherit more clinically ineffective traditions of consultation than in the healthier areas. The availability of good medical care tends to vary inversely with the need of the population to be served'.[4]

The 1979 Royal Commission had some hard things to say about GPs in general and GPs in inner-city areas above all. It wrote that there were 'good reasons to think that standards of competence are not always as high as they might be', and quoted evidence from the Royal College of General Practice which stated: 'Our picture of the assets of good general practice must be balanced by the frank recognition that care by some doctors is mediocre and by a minority is of an unacceptably low standard.' The Royal Commission agreed with what it called an 'admirably candid view'. The services in London caused particular concern: 'In some declining urban areas and in particular in parts of London, the NHS is failing dismally to provide an adequate primary care service to its patients.'

Very little appears to have changed but this is deceptive and hospital services at district general hospitals are being cut back with the explicit expectation that the primary health care service will fill the gap. There should be a case for positive discrimination, in terms of new resources, in favour of those areas where it is most obviously unable to do so. Unfortunately the NHS does not work like this.

The Administration of GPs

The primary obstacle to co-ordinating hospital and GPs' services is that they are not run by the same organisations. Hospitals are run by health authorities, GPs are administered by family practitioner committees and although they are both part of the NHS they are as different as chalk and cheese. They have different budgets, different constitutions, different bureaucracies and different powers.

The division of responsibility goes back to the years after the last war when the NHS was set up amidst a welter of hostility and opposition from the medical establishment who feared that state medicine would turn them into public employees and compromise their independence. Family doctors were taken on one side and made the proverbial offer that is too good to refuse. Unlike their hospital-based colleagues, who became salaried employees of the Health Service, albeit with considerable freedoms at consultant level, GPs were offered both a regular salary *and* their continued independence. The plan meant setting up a network of regional committees which would 'contract', as the expression has it, with family doctors to provide medical care in their regions. The terms of the contract would enshrine the right of GPs to continue as self-employed professionals, paid by the NHS for the patients they treat and guaranteed a minimum income provided they offer a minimum service. The committees were called executive committees and they are still with us, broadly unchanged, though today they are called family practitioner committees or FPCs. It is a division of responsibility which has had considerable implications for the running of the Health Service ever since.

Family practitioner committees are peculiarly unaccountable bodies. They are empowered to spend large sums of public money without recourse to anybody except themselves and the Secretary of State for Health, who with ninety-eight family practitioner committees in England and Wales to keep track of, not to mention the rest of his job, is a distant and formal figurehead. The family practitioner committee responsible for Haringey spent £30 million of public money in 1985 without reference to any elected body representing either the local community or the national interest. There are representatives of local interests like councils, which have four seats, but the representatives are appointees of the Secretary of State, not delegates of the local population, and there is no chain of direct accountability or responsibility through them to local people. Until quite recently family practitioner committee meetings were usually closed to the general public and although this has changed, such is their low profile that most people still confuse them with the family planning clinic. Nine out of ten people I asked during one day had no idea of their powers, who sits on them or even where they are physically located. Hard as it may be to believe today, in 1948 we effectively delegated responsibility for an enormously important part of the NHS to an administration over which we have virtually no control.

The arrangement means that there is no power in the land which can plan or dictate how GPs choose to practise medicine now or in the future and systematic planned change is almost impossible. GPs are free to choose the hours they work, where and how, within broad limits, their surgeries are conducted and who they treat, even though each of these has significant implications for the quality of primary health care. A recent study in Manchester found that approximately 33 per cent of family doctors spent less than sixteen hours a week seeing patients, 16 per cent spent less than twelve hours a week and one doctor spent as little as five.[5] These figures do not take account of time spent travelling to house calls, paper work, liaising with colleagues who may also have an interest in a patient, or keeping abreast of new developments in medicine, but even if you double the hours to allow for this, 33 per cent are still working less than a thirty-five-hour week. Some probably flesh out the remaining hours on the golf course, but among the doctors I met, many had second, even third, jobs outside the NHS; for example, medical officer to a local employer or supervising doctor at a private rest home for the elderly. This proliferation of employment is not forced on them because they are intrinsically short of money. A doctor with an average number of patients performing an average number of consultations and visits can expect to earn at least £22,000 a year for the twenty-hour week, after allowing for deductible surgery expenses. It is the result of having the freedom to make more.

This independence relegates family practitioner committees to a purely administrative or servicing role. They
cannot determine the local pattern of primary health care or,
more importantly in a time of change, plan its future shape.
They are limited to policing the immediate terms of the
contract which in practice means ensuring that patients
accepted by a doctor and paid for by the NHS are getting
'full and proper' treatment. Broader issues like the distribution of surgeries or the range of services are left, very
largely, to chance.

Many people have said it is an absurdity and there have
been a number of attempts at reform. In 1974 the administration of the NHS was reorganised and the executive
committee system changed to bring it more closely in line
with the rest of the Health Service. The reorganisation set up
today's family practitioner committees which corresponded
to health authority administrative boundaries, and it made
each family practitioner committee dependent on the local
health authority for facilities like accommodation and
administrative services. But closer liaison depended on good
will and voluntary co-operation and like most enforced
relationships there was not much of either. Rudolf Klein
marvelled, at the time, at the political clout of family doctors
which had ensured their continued independence. 'GPs had
successfully asserted their right to veto,' he wrote. 'Their
power was measured in terms of what was not done, because
it was defined to be outside the realm of the politically
feasible.'[6]

Five years later the Royal Commission on the NHS also
found the system an absurdity and recommended that family
practitioner committees should be abolished and their
functions taken over by health authorities so that hospital
and community medicine could be integrated. The Commission said it had received a good deal of evidence that the
complete integration of the NHS was prevented so long as
family practitioner committees retained their independence.
But in 1982 when the Health Service went through another

reorganisation, the recommendation was ignored and family practitioner committees not only regained their freedom, they regained some of the freedoms of the 1948 executive committees, floating completely free from their corresponding health authorities. Klein again gazed in wonder at their political clout. It represented, he wrote,

the acceptance of the fact that an attempt to integrate GPs into the NHS by abolishing family practitioner committees, as recommended by the Royal Commission, would carry excessive political costs by leading to a confrontation with GPs. Once again the medical profession had been able to veto change, not by opposing it explicitly, but by constraining the concept of feasibility held by policy makers.[7]

Yet there is an abundance of evidence which suggests that the family practitioner committee system has dismally failed in an area like Tottenham and today is the major obstacle to change and improvement. While the hospital service is rationalised, the family practitioner committee system means that primary health care is unable to respond or adapt itself in a co-ordinated or appropriate fashion.

The Enfield and Haringey family practitioner committee is at the far end of the Piccadilly tube line at a place called Cockfosters, a green and genteel outer London suburb, a good haul from most parts of Haringey and symbolic of the organisation's traditional remoteness from the people it serves. It is not much frequented by the local population and if many did turn up to the bi-monthly meetings, the room would rapidly overflow; as it is, half the members sit back to back around a U-shaped table because there is no other way to cram them in. It is administered by a helpful and sympathetic Indian called Navarro Colaco who has spent twenty years rising up through the ranks of the Health Service and can now cite chunks of the constitution by heart like others cite poetry; sometimes when he talks you wonder whether he is quoting or it is just his style of delivery. He talks with a dry and resigned humour about his job and the more you hear about it the more you understand why.

The Enfield and Haringey family practitioner committee, as its name implies, does not share common boundaries with the local health authority. But it has never been an organisation which has taken boundaries very seriously. In the early years of the NHS, GPs in the outer areas of north London were administered by a vast octopus of a body called the Middlesex executive committee based at Wembley, which covered the whole of the old county of Middlesex. In 1974 when the Health Service was reorganised, the Middlesex executive committee was broken up on paper into five 'local' family practitioner committees and this should have formed the basis of a firmer and closer working relationship between them and the new area health authorities. But in the case of Haringey it did not work out that way. Enfield and Haringey family practitioner committee got an administrator with an office but what it did not get was an administration to go with it. Money and logistics got in the way and somewhere along the line the original idea of making family practitioner committees more locally responsive got lost. To start off with, the Wembley building had five years of its lease still to go and it seemed, to the powers that be at the time, an expensive folly to give it up early and lose money. So the administration remained at Wembley under the new name of the Brent and Harrow family practitioner committee but essentially the old executive committee. This decision was reinforced by problems in breaking up the huge patient register, which lists doctors and their patients, into the five new family practitioner committee areas; 2.5 million index cards which had to be sorted manually. For more than two years clerks shuffled their way through them but after missing two deadlines, the whole operation was declared too expensive and since the Wembley building still existed it seemed to make sense to retain the whole patient register on one site as before.

The problem was that without a register and with virtually no staff, the Enfield and Haringey administrator, in common with other local administrators in the area, could not do his job. He could not compile an up-to-date list of GPs and their patients, he could not pay GPs and, very importantly, he had great difficulty in dealing with complaints from patients about the quality of the treatment they were getting. Even basic information had to be obtained from Wembley and because staff there were not accountable to him, he usually did not get what he wanted without considerable delay. In 1978 a patient finally despaired after waiting several years to get a complaint resolved and complained to the government's ombudsman, who agreed that the system was unsatisfactory. Enfield and Haringey finally got an administration to go with its administrator. But that still left the finance department, the all-important patient register and the supplies department at Wembley, fourteen miles from Cockfosters. In 1980 it got the finance department, an event which is drily recorded in a background document produced by the family practitioner committee: 'For the past ten years the energies of Enfield and Haringey family practitioner committee have been directed to securing control of the administration of the family practitioner committee services in Enfield and Haringey. In 1978 it managed to gain control of the administration and in 1980 of its finances and ophthalmic departments, but patient records and stores continue to be controlled by staff managed by Brent and Harrow family practitioner committee.'

In April 1985, with the Wembley lease now dead and out of the way, Enfield and Haringey family practitioner committee finally got hold of its records and supply departments, eleven years late. But even this was a partial fiction for some months. The idea had been to put the patient register on computer so that it could be more easily transferred to Cockfosters, but staff once again found that this took longer than expected. Through the spring and early summer of 1985, Enfield and Haringey family practitioner committee had to bus staff the fourteen miles to Wembley and back so that they could work on the incomplete computer files. Navarro Colaco, who is a conscientious and diligent man, could weep as he tells you about it, if it was not all so laughable.

It goes without saying that the adequacy or otherwise of the service received scant attention during this period. There were no routine inspections of surgeries, although a number were known to be sub-standard, and no attempt to provide even the vaguest outline plans for the way services might develop in the future if the area was to have comprehensive cover. Haringey community health council reported that between 1974 and 1980 there was no up-dating of the local list of doctors and that the 1973 list continued to be the only official source of information. There was no information about doctors who had retired, moved their premises or changed their hours and no up-to-date list of the sorts of services doctors provided or the areas they specialised in. It was therefore impossible for local residents to make an informed choice about which GP practice they wanted to sign up with or even to get a sense of the choices available.

Some of this has changed. The family practitioner committee now provides up-to-date information and following legislative changes in 1984 is obliged to plan and monitor more closely what goes on. It is expected to conduct routine inspections, though it prefers the word visit, of surgeries, a power which it had before but seldom used, with muscle to impose financial sanctions if premises are not up to scratch, to broadly plan the development of the services in the district and to produce a publicly available annual report on each year's work. How these new powers will work out has still to be tested. Enfield and Haringey family practitioner committee is well aware that it still needs to tread very carefully and it is a long way from being able to dictate terms or implement plans. New members of the committee are issued with a background paper which warns them that 'whereas health authorities can direct and control finance and manpower, family practitioner committees have to work largely through a process of information, consultation, persuasion and influence to achieve their ends'.

In the absence of serious monitoring the traditional way of ensuring that the public is getting value for money from its doctors has been through a complaints procedure which, as Klein scathingly points out, was 'originated in 1913 and taken over virtually unchanged when the family practitioner committees replaced executive committees' in 1974. It is a long and wearisome procedure which many critics feel is heavily stacked in favour of the medical profession. For most of the period up until the early 1980s, Enfield and Haringey family practitioner committee had a reputation, shared with others, for extreme reluctance in pursuing a complaint, a reluctance which in its case was only partially explained by its administrative feebleness. There has tended to be a belief among family practitioner committees that their job is to defend the medical profession rather than serve the public. This aside, there are two major difficulties with the procedure which have hampered its usefulness. The first revolves around what is understood by a doctor's accountability to his or her patients. This is how Enfield and Haringey's administrator Navarro Calaco explained it:

Our investigations are purely to do with whether a doctor is in breach of the terms of his contract. Very often people will write to us saying my doctor has been negligent. Negligence is a civil tort, it's not something we are empowered to deal with. If a doctor makes a wrong diagnosis, that is not something which is a breach of the terms of his contract; in other words he could kill you. You have got to go elsewhere to complain about that, not to us. A common complaint is rudeness; the attitude and behaviour of doctors. That's not something I can do anything about. But, and this is the important wording, if he didn't *put himself in a position* to arrive at a correct diagnosis, that is a breach of the terms of his service.

This is not an easy concept to pin down as Mr Calaco goes on to explain. 'Suppose you complain because a doctor has refused you a home visit. The doctor can argue that on the basis of his clinical judgement and the information available, it wasn't necessary to make a visit and so long as he has asked the patient the appropriate questions and is in a position to make a decision, he's in the clear. Clinical judgement is not a matter we can investigate.' But of course a good deal can rest on clinical judgement and it is a big hole for the medical profession to climb through.

The second problem is that the process grinds exasperatingly slowly. Navarro Colaco described how it works:

A patient writes to say my doctor refused to visit me. I would ensure that the patient is registered with that doctor. I would then send copies of the letter to the chairman of the medical services committee [which deals with complaints and is half composed of doctors]. The chairman would decide whether there were reasonable grounds for a complaint and if there isn't we would tell the patient. But if there are grounds for a complaint I would send it to the doctor concerned and ask for his comments. These comments would go to the patient to see if he has further comments and when we have got all this it goes back to the chairman who decides when to have a hearing or whether it can be dealt with by correspondence.

If there is a hearing it goes to the full medical services committee. The committee has a number of sanctions open to it if it believes a doctor is in breach of his or her contract. It can issue a warning, make a penal withholding (a fine), recommend a reduction in a doctor's list size or, as a last resort, decide to remove the doctor from the register, a move which means the doctor can no longer practice. When the decision has been made, copies go to the patient, the doctor and the Secretary of State. There is a right of appeal to the Secretary of State and the case is finalised when the Secretary of State has given a judgement. All this takes six to eight months and if there is an appeal nearer to eighteen. The average time in Haringey in 1983 was twelve months.

The effect of these difficulties has been to severely limit the number of people who have bothered to make use of the procedure. A study in the 1970s discovered that during one entire year, family practitioner committees in England only received 540 complaints.[8] Of these about half were dismissed without a hearing on the grounds that they were 'frivolous, vexatious or disclosed no prima facie grounds of breach of service', and altogether 453 cases were decided in favour of the doctor. The author concluded: 'In the event, during a not untypical year, there were 91 cases – about one per 225 GPs – in which a complaint about professional negligence was established. It's hard to accept that any service performed by human beings can be so immune from criticism.'

In Haringey there has been a recent improvement in the family practitioner committee's sensitivity towards complaints with the result that they have gone up quite markedly. This is illustrated in the table below. But there is still an enormous amount of confusion. In 1984 nearly thirty complaints out of a total of sixty-two were dismissed or returned on the basis that they were inappropriate or irrelevant. The DHSS is currently consulting with the medical profession about ways of improving on this, but nobody expects anything very dramatic to come out of it.

Feb 1982–June 1983	Dental	3 hearings
July 1983–Dec 1984	Dental	7 hearings
Feb 1982–June 1983	Pharmacy	No cases
July 1983–Dec 1984	Pharmacy	6 hearings
Feb 1982–June 1983	med services	7 letters; 6 hearings
July 1983–Dec 1984	med services	14 letters; 15 hearings

(Enfield and Haringey family practitioner committee)

Nor are there very great hopes for the new planning powers of family practitioner committees. The most important single influence over the number of GPs in an area remains a very crude procedure set up in 1948. In the early days of the Health Service the government and medical profession realised that if doctors were given a free hand to choose where they worked there would be a most undignified scramble for the more prosperous and desirable parts of the country where there would be fierce competition for patients, while less attractive areas would be in the opposite situation. Nobody would benefit from it. It was therefore decided to set up an obscure body called the medical practices committee, charged with the task of trying to ensure a relatively even distribution of doctors across the country. To this end it divided the country into four categories:

Restricted. Adequately doctored; average list size less than 1,700 per capita. Very unlikely that somebody could set up a new practice but could get a new partner.

Intermediate. Adequately doctored. Average list size 1,701 to 2,100. Might get a new practice.

Open. Inadequately doctored. Average list size 2,101 to 2,500. More doctors needed. New applicants automatically accepted.

Designated. Over 2,500. Much less than adequately doctored. Special allowance to attract doctors. Only two in the country.

These categories still stand. Twice a week the medical practices committee meets in London to hear applications from doctors who want to set up a new practice and by and large, it decides whether they should or should not be allowed to on the basis of the designation of area concerned. But it's a purely negative control which prevents new doctors moving into areas already considered adequately doctored but has no power to direct them to under-provided areas. Financial incentives are available for 'designated' areas but there are only two of these in the country and there is no positive incentive to move to an 'open' area. Furthermore the categories are based on a simple head count; they have nothing to do with the quality or range of services offered and a good practice with a wide range of clinics and services counts for exactly the same as a practice which provides a basic surgery and limited hours. It is a crude and negative procedure which takes little or no account of variations *within* an area, and areas from the point of view of this classification can be quite large.

Enfield and Haringey, which until recently has not had an up-to-date patient register, and therefore no detailed information on how adequate the number of doctors is for the population, has for many years been a restricted area, a classification which has prevented new blood moving in and largely fossilised the existing range of provision. In 1986 this marginally altered. The long overdue, up-dated, patient register showed, what many people had known for a long time, that the average list size in the area was higher than expected and the classification has been altered to 'intermediate'. But this is unlikely to make a great deal of difference. Although it will now be possible to marginally increase the number of doctors in the area, traditionally under-doctored inner-city areas like Tottenham continue to lack any positive inducement or method of persuasion which will enable it to attract new blood. South Tottenham, which recently lost the accident and emergency department at the Prince of Wales hospital, remains a black hole, an area which, in the words of the family practitioner committee's 1985–86 annual report, has 'fewer doctors than is desirable from the point of view of patient choice and ease of access', and for groups of patients like the elderly, handicapped, mothers with children, 'the existence of major roads or the lack of personal or suitable public transport, can present real barriers to their use of doctors' services'. South Tottenham is carved up by major roads. The family practitioner committee is sympathetic to the problem and willing to make out a case for more doctors in this patch, but the problem is inducing them to go there.

Even these relatively minor increases in family practitioner committee influence are viewed with misgiving by a Tottenham doctor like Harry Wallace. He looks at the marginal increase in their power, at the prospect of routine visits, and the idea of voluntary planning guidelines and wants no part of it. 'I don't really want to be dictated to by some bureaucrat who probably isn't qualified,' he scoffs.

I had a lot of problems in the services with people trying to tell me what to do and not to do. When they weren't doctors I didn't take very kindly to them. As for today's bureaucrats, some I like and some I don't. Some try to tell you ABC and they are really boring people. But I can feel that there is the beginning of a squeeze on the profession. The minister (of health) doesn't like it – all ministers don't like the fact that we have been independent contractors. My vocation has always been the care of the sick. I don't really want to be dictated to by some bureaucrat. Unfortunately I see the face of general practice becoming much more bureaucratically orientated.

Thus speaks the authentic voice of medicine, a voice which has said roughly the same for the last forty years and which has carried all before it. It has encouraged the family practitioner committee system to perpetuate a small privileged group of people and a fragmented Health Service and the sad thing is that those most in need of monitoring and planning are the least likely to accept it.

Meanwhile in the absence of more meaningful activity, an enormous amount of the energy of family practitioner committees is devoted to ensuring the smooth running of an arcane and Byzantine payments system, based on a form of piecework. The system starts with what is called a basic practice allowance, which every doctor with more than 1,000 patients on his or her list is entitled to. To this is added extra money for seniority, vocational training (in obstetrics or geriatrics for instance) or for being part of a group practice. On top of this comes what is called a capitation fee, based on a breakdown of patients by age; you get more for the very young and old. There are additional payments for out-of-hours responsibilities like night visits. And this is just the basic wage. The second part of the wage comes from what are known as 'items of service' payments, twelve of them, ranging from emergency visits to cervical smears. Each GP submits periodic returns to the family practitioner committee for his or her 'items of service' payments and each of these has to be checked. 'It is public money after all,' says Mr Colaco,

There is no way we are going to accept everything they send. We need to check that they satisfy the criteria laid down in the book. For example, we may get a claim for a night visit or an emergency call out. The first thing we want to check is, is that patient registered with you for the service and if not we want to know from the patient why she [sic] didn't get her own doctor. The usual answer will be, 'well, my doctor wasn't available.' We would then write to the doctor asking why he wasn't available. If we are satisfied by his answer, then we will deduct cash from that doctor and give it to the one who made the visit. We don't see why the NHS should pay twice.

Quite so, but surely there must be a simpler, more efficient way of doing it. In almost any other walk of life piecework and bonuses have long ago been bought out in the name of value for money and simplicity.

Inevitably a system like this costs money which counts against the overall NHS budget. Enfield and Haringey family practitioner committee spent £634,000 on administrative costs in 1985, while across at the local health authority the community health budget was being cut by £70,000 a year and there is a very serious shortage of health visitors. A smoother, less bureaucratic payment system would probably release enough cash to make up the entire shortage of health visitors with enough over to avoid the £70,000 annual cut. When other parts of the Health Service are being minutely scrutinised for inefficiency and waste it is a little strange that family practitioner committees should be allowed to remain so blatantly wasteful and inefficient. The surely unnecessary and excessive costs of administering the family practitioner services is just one reminder that we are still paying dearly for the 1948 deal.

The terms of reference within which family practitioner committees operate mean that even today they cannot run the family practitioner service in a way which is likely to ensure that the public gets a comprehensive or even adequate service. It is therefore not surprising that despite the number of studies which have shown that deprived working-class areas like Tottenham have worse GP services than better-off areas like Highgate, nothing has been done about it. Nothing can be done about it unless GPs themselves individually choose to do it and in an inner-city area like Tottenham that is unlikely to happen. While Tottenham's hospitals close down, the family practitioner service remains the same.

The Community Health Service

There have been suggestions that district health authorities should compensate for this by selectively developing their own community health services. Several years ago Haringey community health council drew attention to the imbalance in primary health care between the east and west parts of the district and suggested a policy of positive discrimination in favour of those areas where the numbers and scope of GPs were poorest. Many members of the health authority are sympathetic to the idea and the authority, as a whole, broadly shares a conviction that if something new is to be done, the east should be given first consideration. But it is not firm enough to be called a 'policy' and it is unlikely ever to become one.

The health authority has a community services unit which is responsible for running and developing the district's community health programme; it runs clinics and health centres and the community staff who work in and from them: district nurses, health visitors and community para-medical staff like speech therapists and chiropodists. It runs screening programmes for women and children and a domiciliary nursing service for the elderly. In a profile which it gives out to the interested public the district describes itself as having 'well advanced' community services and some are exceptional. It has a pioneering community audiology department which has celebrated its fiftieth birthday and is recognised throughout the region as being outstanding. For many years it employed one of the few community psychiatrists in the country and the community dental service is well thought of. Many of these services run in tandem with the family practitioner services and even in some cases from the same building. They back up and complement each other and between them provide what is known as the primary or community health care service.

But community services generally have traditionally been accorded a low priority with correspondingly uncertain funding, and much of the rest of the provision is patchy and threadbare. The unit has inherited an appalling legacy of old and crumbling clinics, many of which should have been replaced or demolished years ago. One is virtually derelict, the upstairs floors declared unfit for human habitation. Two others are in temporary premises, one an aging prefab, the other a large house which was taken over when the original clinic fell down, and is described by the health authority as 'very unsuitable'. Yet another is on the first floor of an old school hall and is reached by a steep external iron staircase, and some of the difficulties in overcoming them, are highlighted by the abject failure of the health centre development where they are temporarily housed in a large windowless barracks at the back of the empty building. A less inviting place would be hard to find.

The weaknesses of the community health care programme, and some of the difficulties in overcoming them, are highlighted by the abject failure of the health centre development policy, where a combination of poor funding and the sheer structural problem of co-ordinating the two wings of the service have left it a shadow of what it might have been.

Health centres have been seen as an important route to improving community care for forty years. The term has been liberally applied over time to everything from clinics to surgeries and has become virtually meaningless, but the original conception was of NHS funded centres which pulled together GPs and community health staff (district nurses, health visitors and so on) under one roof to provide a more comprehensive range of services than the average surgery or clinic could ever hope to emulate. They offer health authorities the opportunity to create major concentrations of community resources and provide one of the few bridges between family practitioner committees and the rest of the service. The hope has always been that the NHS, in the shape of district health authorities, would seize on them as a mechanism for galvanising community health care and overcoming the vagaries of the family practitioner committee system. 'It seems to us that health centres offer several advantages,' wrote the Royal Commission on the NHS. 'They can set standards, they can make it easier to experiment with different methods of providing care and they can house a wide range of services . . . In our view they can significantly improve the quality and access of services to patients.'[9]

So much for the idea; the development programme has never taken off. The DHSS and regional health authorities have proved surprisingly reluctant to finance them – a change in national funding policy in the mid-1970s means building grants are only available in designated inner-city areas – and GPs have frequently remained wary of becoming involved with a programme they do not control and which has occasionally fulfilled their worst expectations of bureaucratic ineptitude.

Haringey should have four new health centres today, nothing perhaps to shout about, but better than the two-and-a-half it has actually got. In the 1960s plans were drawn up for health centres in Tottenham, Wood Green, Bounds Green and Crouch End, but almost from the beginning they hit problems. The Tottenham centre, arguably the strategically most important, never got past the planning stage. Initially it got tangled up in a bureaucratic muddle about where exactly it should be and by the time this had been resolved, the alteration in national funding policy pulled the finances from under it. Tottenham is not designated an 'inner city' area and the project was still-born.

The Bounds Green centre, in the west of the district, moved ahead more rapidly and was just in time to escape the inner-city ruling. But once built it was unable to recruit GPs to work in it. The health centre had been built to accommodate six, but for the first two years none could be persuaded to leave their existing premises and move in and it operated as a glorified clinic and base for district nurses and other community staff. Gradually over a four-year period doctors trickled in in ones and twos until they reached five which is where it has remained ever since. The health authority has abandoned hope of filling the last place.

Several years later the saga was repeated when the Crouch End health centre opened with space for eight doctors. The Crouch End centre had fallen foul of the DHSS inner-city ruling and, languishing for several years on the drawing board for lack of funds, took over ten years to complete. During this protracted gestation doctors initially interested gave up in despair and found alternative accommodation so that when the centre finally opened, only one could be found to move in. For eighteen months he practised in splendid isolation and the spare accommodation was once again filled with district community staff. He was then joined by a second doctor and some months later by a third, but two years after the centre had opened there were still only three in a building designed for eight. The number has now been downgraded and extra clinics added because, as one administrator put it, 'we realised there wasn't a cat's chance in hell of getting eight doctors and the building was being underused'. The only health centre opened in anything approaching a planned manner has been Wood Green, built in the 1960s when funds were still to be had. It is a pretty shaky track record which exposes serious structural problems with the procedure for building and getting them off the ground and has left many local GPs, wary anyway, relieved that they have had nothing to do with them. 'There are some very unhappy health centres round here,' I was informed by one slightly self-satisfied Tottenham doctor.

'I'm glad we had nothing to do with them. We put our money where our mouth was and built our own. We own it, we dictate the terms of what happens. In a health centre which is owned by the health authority *they* can dictate the terms; how much you have to pay and who is employed and you don't have the least say in the matter.' For some they still smack of a salaried profession and the loss of 'independent contractor' status; for others they are merely the apotheosis of what goes wrong when a project is poorly managed and badly funded. Stories of light bulbs which take two months to be replaced or the probably apocryphal fifteen phone calls to get the door of a consulting room to shut properly, ring all too true and they prefer to go their own way. Almost certainly the most progressive health centre in the district is a privately-owned one in Highgate.

Some of these structural problems should be on the verge of a solution. The rationalisation and streamlining of the acute hospital service has been accompanied by an explicit commitment to make community services a priority area for new funds and some of the separate programmes which make it up, like screening for cervical and breast cancer, have even been individually singled out for special attention. The NHS's community health programme should be about to enter a period of growth, if not prosperity, and it is open to health authorities to ignore, to some degree, the whims and fancies of the family practitioner committee system and to expand their own community programmes through clinics and domiciliary services which visit people in their homes.

But how far this can happen depends on the annual allocation of funds to the NHS and we know, in RAWP-losing parts of the country, this does not look very promising. 'We are talking, as a matter of national and local policy, of developing services in the community, which most dictricts are able to do,' I was told by Dot Spence, Haringey community service's administrator in the mid-1980s.

We *are* developing community services here, but in such a small way. Most districts are prioritising their community services; we are having more difficulty. I have been told I have got to save £70,000 this year [1986–87] bearing in mind that I have saved £70,000 for the last three years and out of a budget of £4.5 million there is a limit to how many £70,000s you can take. We have done it up to now and we will do it this year, but next year I have said 'sorry chums, we have come to the end of the road.' Either I lose ten bodies [which incidentally gives some idea of NHS pay levels] and we have already shaved down and shaved down and I have cut administrative staff to what we actually need, or we rationalise the premises we have got.

EXPENDITURE ON COMMUNITY SERVICES AS A PERCENTAGE OF TOTAL BUDGET (less admin) (£ million)

	1976/7	1977/8	1978/9	1979/80	1980/1	1985/6
Hospital	14.548	16.162	17.548	20.450	26.642	41.000
Community	1.522	1.701	1.964	2.381	3.203	4.500
%	10.5	10.5	10.1	10.4	10.7	10.0

(Haringey district health authority)

In other words the community budget, although a priority area, remains extremely tight and any expansion will have to come primarily from the rationalisation of what is already there; in a RAWP-losing district there is no new money for the priority services. What is more, whatever funds can be released, will have to make good past neglect as well as finance new services. It is an open question whether it will be able to meet this double task and, equally importantly, do so without spreading resources so thinly that standards fall. In a RAWP-losing district like Haringey this last point is gradually emerging as one of the crunch issues. The health authority is hoping to squeeze some £200,000 a year, for the next few years, out of the district-wide cost improvement exercise and the rationalisation of acute hospital beds, to assist the development of the community programme. Some of this money is likely to come from value-for-money exercises applied to the existing community services. It is this unspecified sum which is causing some observers concern. Their worry is that in the name of value for money, the character of some community services themselves will be altered in a manner which raises bigger questions than value-for-money exercises are qualified to cope with. Two areas of the community programme, in particular, look to managers like candidates for rationalisation. The first is the developmental screening programme for children.

Many health authorities have already rationalised their routine developmental checks for children over the age of five on the grounds that they are no longer necessary in the late twentieth century. Haringey is following suit. Dot Spence, who in her time as community unit administrator backed the idea, explained the thinking behind the move.

The prevention we have done in the past is not necessarily what is appropriate now for children, because of changes in social conditions. We used to be looking for malnutrition, but what we are looking for now is handicap. This will only occur in a small proportion of the population and you therefore don't need to screen every well child to find it. Moreover we know much more about the development of handicapping conditions in children. We know that if a kid is going to develop a handicap, it will probably develop by the age of five and therefore you need to put in a fairly intensive screening programme from 0 to 5, but after that you can let up. The change we are making is that we used to send doctors into schools when kids were as old as 14 to look for hearing and visual problems. But there is nothing a doctor is going to pick up seeing a kid at that age that a health visitor or mum or GP is not going to find.

Not everybody agrees. Critics like Councillor Maureen Dewar, a Labour Party appointee on the health authority, believe this is an oversimplification and that in areas like Tottenham and parts of Wood Green and Stroud Green, where there is considerable economic deprivation, it is still important to check that children, even quite old ones, are being properly fed and looked after. They are doubtful that teachers, who are also under immense pressure with thirty or so children in a class, will pick up problems, especially if they are among children from the ethnic minorities, and they have equally little confidence in the ability of GPs to catch health problems that may not be immediately obvious.

Beyond this, their fear is that rationalising one area of the community service, however innocent it may seem in its own right, will gradually and perhaps imperceptibly narrow the definition of what community health care should be. These fears come to a head over talk of rationalising Haringey's network of decaying clinics. Community unit managers are convinced that streamlining these ramshackle and inappropriate premises would both save money and provide a better service. They argue that there is no logic to the current geographical pattern of clinics, that many are in old, inefficient and unsuitable buildings and that some are unpleasant to be in and underused. Their preferred solution, I was told, would be to close many down, making substantial savings in running costs, and centralise the service at a number of the better existing premises and perhaps some new ones, with possibly a series of part-time branch clinics sharing staff with them. But the closure of clinics is a political hot potato in some parts of the district and the authority is pursuing these thoughts with some caution. Eight years ago it got its fingers burnt when it threatened to close the badly decaying Stroud Green clinic after a burst water pipe rendered the elderly premises virtually uninhabitable. The threat stirred up an embarrassingly vociferous local campaign. The authority maintained that a new health centre was about to be opened in Crouch End, only fifteen minutes' walk away. The campaign pointed out that it was twenty-five minutes' walk up a steep hill; the administration countered that this did not matter because the clinic was primarily catering for 'young mothers and not old-age pensioners'; the campaign responded that the clinic was actually catering for small children, and women offered to lend them to the district administrator so that he could try out the walk for himself. The authority backed down.

Today what stirs up opponents of this rationalisation programme is a belief that a pattern of large and centralised clinics and health centres is not only less convenient, but that their size begins to affect the quality of the service they offer. Above all they run the risk of becoming as impersonal and institutional as any hospital outpatients department. This does not matter if all you are doing is providing medical care in the narrow sense – medical problems diagnosed and treated – but community medicine should have a broader definition.

Like primary health care, should it not also concern itself with prevention, education and the 'whole' person and, where family practitioner committee services are poor, should it not be easily available so that people can drop in as they would at a surgery? In this debate views become quickly polarised. Dot Spence, with her brisk and efficient administrator's hat firmly on her head, goes for the narrow definition, perhaps pushed by her intimate awareness of the financial constraints under which the service is operating. 'I feel we are misusing our staff by having a drop-in centre. Although health visitors may be able to help they are being used as social workers and although it's a hard thing to say, that's not really our business.'

The opposition profoundly disagree. 'To call it social work is to demean the health visitor,' maintains Maureen Dewar. 'Health visitors can often do more than the social worker because they know the patients better, they are closer to them. Instead of contracting health visitors' support they should be putting more in and using clinics more fully.' There is an awareness that with a little more money clinics of all kinds could be better used and more closely tied to the life of a neighbourhood. Most clinics are never used in the evening although clubs for handicapped people, the elderly, stroke victims and so on, desperately need support and premises. Haringey cannot afford the extra caretakers to staff the buildings in the evenings and anyway, most of the clinics are so drab, nobody in their right mind would want to hold a social activity in one. It is a matter of money, but it is also a matter of vision. What worries the authority's critics is that even if it had the vision in the first place, it is now allowing financial considerations to cloud its judgement and the long-term result will be an impoverishment of the community health service, in the name of efficiency, at a time when it needs to be enriched.

The irony of this dilemma is not lost on the community administration who, while anxious to save money, are aware of the pressures on the service they are providing and how close to the wind they are sailing. 'They are chucking people out of hospital and they are cutting my budget,' says Dot Spence.

It cannot go on. We don't know what the knock-on effect of rationalising hospitals is on the community services because we don't have the information about what we are doing now, so it's absolutely impossible to get information on how it is going to affect us in the future. But we do know the work load has increased. We do know that district nurses are doing more treatments. The real effect, I think, is that we have got more high tech patients in the community. Whereas ten years ago the nurses spent their time doing injections and bandages and that sort of thing, they are now having the multiple handicapped; the quadriplegic who is at home with a family and who needs to be lifted and turned. We may have to send two nurses in. The baby that Barts [St Bartholomew's] or UCH [University College Hospital] miraculously saves becomes our responsibility. The heroics of the teaching hospital has this dreadful knock-on effect where we have to provide maybe a couple of nurses a day and the technology as well. We are saving the hospitals money, we are picking up the tab, but our budget is decreasing at the same time. And at some point it's going to burst.

She has had great difficulty convincing her colleagues of the seriousness of the problems because of a dearth of hard management information about what community staff do and what kind of patients they have. The pressure of their work load and the adequacy with which they can do their job only emerge at times of crisis when something breaks down, at which point it is usually easier to scapegoat the individual than revamp the system. Dot Spence explained:

We haven't got real information on what our district nurses are doing and how we are using them. We get activity sheets saying what they do each day but unless you have got a more patient-based information system which tells you who is suffering from what and what their level of dependency is and you can tie that in with the visits of the district nurses, you have got no real idea of what these people are doing. The amount of information we have on community services is minimal. We employ six physiotherapists. I don't know what the hell they do; I don't know how many visits they do or what level of work they have. There is no way of knowing what these people are doing.

You can see the district nurses are doing more but there is no way of telling what exactly they are doing. If you have got a ward with twenty-five people in it you can tell exactly what each nurse does; we got the patients up, we bathed them, six went to theatre and so on. There is a lot of information on hospitals. But the community services, from a nursing point of view, has always been seen as not costing much so it doesn't matter very much if we haven't got a handle on what is going on. It's only now that people are beginning to develop information packages for the community and we in Haringey are a long way from being able to afford them.

Better information would require a mini-computer and somebody to operate and look after it, a minimum outlay, I was told, of £100,000 and Haringey's community unit is a long, long way from having that kind of sum to spare on what many still consider a relative luxury.

'I have looked,' said Dot Spence, 'at things like how many baths were being done five years ago and how many are being done now and there are a lot of people out there being bathed by us today. There are nurses who if you look at their daily sheet are doing six to eight baths a day; how the hell they can get round their patch in an eight-and-a-half hour day and do that number of baths, beats me. That's some bathing because you can't walk into an elderly person's home and say "right, in/out". To begin which you may have to get hot water and that can take time.'

A crude breakdown of some of the figures shows that

while the number of staff remained broadly constant, between the last half of 1984 and the first half of 1985 (the latest period for which figures are available) new patients increased from 1,701 to 2,780, over 1,000.[10] The figures also show that community medical staff were having to deal with more complicated problems; visits lasting over an hour increased by over a hundred and many patients were having to be seen more frequently. Significantly the number of people over sixty-five being visited also increased – by 4,000 from 65,944 to 69,995 – suggesting what while 'high tech' patients, who might previously not have lived or would have spent longer in hospital, may be an important part of the increased work load, the growing number of elderly people living 'in the community' is also having an impact. Together they reveal a much more dependent population now living at 'home' than ever before. The community services need more of almost every kind of staff. Dot Spence, who was a victim of the Griffiths reshuffle and left in 1986, said that during her time shortages of money had prevented her from recruiting a wide range of staff she knew were needed. She could not increase the number of health visitors to what she knew was a safe and necessary level as far as this sort of inner-urban district is concerned, and although there are enough district nurses by national standards, there are not enough to cope with the run-down of hospitals. 'I also know there are not enough staff like speech therapists because we have a waiting list for kids that we cannot treat before the age of five, which is when we like to catch them.'

In 1986 the DHSS issued a consultative document on the future development of the primary health care service. It was called simply *Primary Health Care: An Agenda for Discussion*, although it was more colloquially referred to as the Green Paper on primary health care, 'green paper' being the traditional phrase for a government discussion document.[11] Government ministers underlined the fact that it was the first time in the history of the Health Service that these services had been comprehensively reviewed. It started from the belief that, as a press release put it, 'despite major advances in recent years, there are still considerable variations in standards provided by GPs'. But the measures it proposed almost entirely miss the central issues of concern. While the real issues are about control and resources, the review confined itself to tinkering with the administration of the service.

Primary health care faces a number of severe problems. To begin with, demand for the service is increasing. Population statistics suggest that there is a growing proportion of the general population which is dependent on others for survival. This increase is partially made up from an increase in the proportion of elderly and very elderly people in society and partly from the growing number of mentally and physically handicapped people who fifteen years ago might have died at birth but are now capable of surviving thanks to advances in medical treatment. These groups are growing in both relative and absolute terms and depend substantially on the health and welfare services for support in continuing to survive.

At one time this demand might have been shared between the hospital and community services but the policy of community care means that most of this demand now comes to rest at the door of the primary health care or community services. An increasing dependent population is turning to a decreasing range of health provision for help. On top of this, the greater concentration in hospitals on curing and productivity means that more people than ever before are being discharged from hospital before they are fit and are turning to the community services to support them through their convalescence.

This increased demand is not evenly spread across the country. Areas of economic and social well-being are more likely to be able to look after their dependent populations than more economically depressed and deprived areas; families and relatives are more likely to have the resources to support and care for somebody and there is more likely to be a thriving charitable and voluntary network. Thus the greatest demand will be concentrated in those areas where the evidence suggests that primary health care services are the least adequate: inner-city and working-class neighbourhoods. We are back to Tudor Hart's Inverse Care Law. A patchy service faces the greatest increase in demand where it is most vulnerable. These pressures suggest that health authorities need to face up to two problems: resources and their distribution. But in grappling with these issues district authorities are seriously hampered by their restricted control over both. Haringey health district's sphere of competence is restricted to hospitals in the east of the district and a limited range of community facilities across the borough as a whole. It has no control over hospitals in the west of the borough and no control over the range and spread of GP services. This severely limits its ability to produce a coherent, planned response. A major chunk of the local service is simply outside its control. This in turn is aggravated by severe restrictions on its resources. Most of the money available for developing community provision will have to be skimmed off the hospital service. This means there is not much around and many of the shortcomings identified by Dot Spence are unlikely to be made good. The authority has been forced to pick out some areas for growth knowing that they are at the expense of others. Thus it has chosen, under public and DHSS pressure, to put some of its scarce resources into an experimental cervical cancer screening facility and recall programme. But it has had to confine this to women in the highest risk category, those over thirty-five, leaving the rest of Haringey's female population to make do as best they can. Yet cervical cancer is the sixth biggest killer in the district which claimed seventy lives in 1983 (latest figures). It has also had to indefinitely postpone plans to introduce a universal breast cancer screening service although breast cancer claimed fifty lives in 1983, and it does very little indeed to combat heart disease although it is the biggest killer in the district with over 500 victims in 1983.[12] Skimming the hospital service also means that far from there being a policy of positive discrimination in favour of those areas of the borough where there is greatest need and demand, there is likely to be a net flow of funds from the east, where there are hospitals, to the west, where Haringey does not control any but still needs to put money into new community provision. Positive discrimination would mean holding down community services in the west so that those in the east could expand more rapidly. But this would mean deliberately developing the east at the expense of the west and since neither are up to scratch this is not considered politically acceptable by the authority. Positive discrimination becomes academic.

Also, in trying to square the circle the health district is falling back on the managerial approach which it has applied in hospitals. This, if anything, is even less appropriate when applied to primary health care. In the name of efficiency it is emphasising the quantifiable and so narrowing the focus of community health provision.

One of the more glaring anomalies in all this is that while health authorities are severely restrained, family practitioner committees continue to enjoy open-ended, unrestricted budgets. The argument runs that GPs are the front line of the Health Service and it is impossible to predict demand for their services. This is not entirely convincing. Similar arguments could be advanced in favour of open-ended budgets for the rest of the primary health care service – district nurses and community midwives for instance – and for hospital doctors who cannot predict the work load coming into a hospital through the casualty department or referred to them by GPs themselves.

But what makes the inequality in funding extraordinary is that the most unaccountable and unplanned area of the Health Service is also the most liberally funded. In some areas and practices GPs may well use it to provide a comprehensive local service, but these, by definition, are the better and more committed practices and tend, as we have seen, not to be in the areas of greatest need. There is a glaring discrepancy in the way the two arms of the service are being treated and while there can be serious reservations about the way health authorities are employing their powers to curtail and restrict funds, it does not follow that the alternative is an open-handed largesse.

The government's consultative document on primary health care is only the latest in a long line of reports which suggest that the family practitioner committee system continues to provide a very uneven service. It seems extraordinary in these circumstances, and while the rest of the Health Service is severely restrained, that it should continue to enjoy a free flow of funds unhampered by any requirements for greater public accountability or closer co-ordination with the rest of the Health Service. It is difficult to escape the conclusion that, once again, GPs are being treated as special cases.

On the major issues of control and funds, the government's discussion document is silent. Instead of facing up to them, it confines itself to minor administrative topics like the age of retirement for family doctors and how they can be encouraged to seek out new patients. This is all the more surprising because the role of the primary health care service has never been more important. It is not only our first line of approach to the Health Service, it is also becoming an essential part of the back-up system which underpins the rest of the service. The rationalisation of hospitals and the spread of community care is based on the primary care services expanding to take up the new demand. This is all the more important because, as the next chapter demonstrates, the policy of caring for an increasing number of dependent people in 'the community', rather than in hospital, is suffering from severe problems of its own.

CHAPTER FIVE

Community Care or Community Neglect

Eileen Thomas is a courageous if prickly old lady of eighty-nine who puts a high price on her independence and, at the moment, is paying a high price for it. She lives in a small, second floor flat on a 1930s council estate not far from the Tottenham football ground; there are faded family snaps on the walls, porcelain animals on the sideboard and large-print library books on the table. During a football match, when the wind is in the right direction, she can hear the roar of the crowd and smell the pungent smell of a dozen hot-dog stalls lined up along the litter-strewn high street; familiar sensations which she is anxious to hold on to. But there are difficulties. Some months ago she fell and fractured a knee and in doing so precipitated a series of events which illustrate painfully clearly the limitations of current community services. It is a saga of repeated hospital treatments and rapid discharges – four in so many months – which have physically and emotionally aged her beyond recognition. She has been caught in what is known as the revolving door syndrome. In each case she has been released from hospital, admittedly at her own request, before she has been able to manage for herself and in each case the local community services have been too stretched to give her sufficient help and support to enable her to live safely and satisfactorily at home alone. The transition is too large and too rapid and she has bounced from hospital to home and back again in ever-decreasing spirals. Each decision is made on the grounds of immediate expediency with responsibility rapidly passing from one authority to another and with no one agency able or willing to halt the process and plan, with her, a more stable, long-term future. The hospital is anxious to maintain its bed throughput and the social service department is statutorily obliged but physically unable to pick up the bits.

This chapter looks at how the Health Service is shaping up to the challenge of providing a civilised service for that section of the population which is dependent on other people for support and help in leading a reasonable and decent life. It is about the Health Service as a caring rather than curing service; about social rather than medical intervention. It is about services for people like Mrs Thomas, the 'elderly' – not a designation they may be very happy with themselves, but generally taken to be people over the age of seventy-five – and others who need continuing long-term care and support, such as those suffering from chronic mental illness, mental handicap or physical disability. They used to be known as the long-stay services; today, ever since the publication by the Labour government in 1976 of the Priorities document, they are more commonly known as the priority or caring services. Often they have got very little to do with medicine. The Health Service has not traditionally been good at this area of health care and the neglect has left us with a legacy of poor and inappropriate facilities which have been demanding, with increasing insistence, attention and remedy. Neither is it an area which sits comfortably beside the new management ideals of throughput and productivity, and dependent people have been hard hit by the hospital rationalisation programme because they do not fit into it.

For these reasons, the NHS is currently committed to an extensive overhaul of provision for dependent people. They have been designated a priority area for new resources and the NHS is heavily backing a non-institutional, community based form of care summed up by that familiar and all-embracing phrase 'community care'. The result is a major upheaval far bigger than anything which is happening in the acute hospitals; indeed, it is probably the biggest single change in service, as opposed to administrative, terms facing the Health Service today. Major hospitals with over 1,000 long-term patients are being closed. Staff who have spent their entire careers in hospital settings are being asked to retrain so that they can work in the new community units. Patients who have lived for up to fifty years on a hospital ward are being rehabilitated to enable them to return to 'the community' and the elderly infirm like Mrs Thomas, who might previously have disappeared for the rest of her life into a hospital for geriatric people, are being encouraged to stay at home. It is an enormous challenge, made bigger still by the considerable speed at which it is being implemented. Local health authorities have been given a timetable for introducing the changes and, like a time bomb, it is galvanising them into quite unusual activity. Not surprisingly, given the size and significance of the change, it has been surrounded by controversy. The abstract principle of community care as a pattern of future provision is generally accepted, but there has been, and continues to be, enormous uncertainty about its implementation and ultimate shape; about what exactly it is and how exactly it will happen. What does it mean to close a large, long-stay, psychiatric hospital and will the replacement facilities, if they ever actually happen, really be any different?

Institutional and Community Care

Haringey is not a good place in which to be old or dependent unless you can afford to supplement the scanty state provision with private facilities. This not my judgement; it is the view of a senior member of the district health authority who is conscious that the health authority today provides a very minimal level of services for these disadvantaged groups of people. It is in no way unique in this, or even particularly blameworthy. Like the rest of the country it has simply failed to give them much thought in the past and has never provided more than the rudiments of care within its own geographical boundaries. Above all, this is true of services for the mentally ill and handicapped and the backbone of this provision, such as it is, continues to be provided by the vast Victorian institutions which ring the outer fringes of large towns and cities like London and pull in patients from huge surrounding catchment areas. There is Friern Barnet, a mile or so north east of Haringey in the outer London borough of Barnet, built in the late 1800s to house 3,000 psychiatric patients and still a major centre of psychiatric care for people living in a wide sweep of north London including west Haringey. It is close compared with Claybury, some fifteen miles to the east out by the M11 motorway, with a similar bed capacity and catering for mentally ill people from all over north east London including Tottenham and east Haringey. Much further out, well beyond the London fringe, there is South Ockenden, near Tilbury in Essex, which until recently took mentally handicapped people from Tottenham, and Harperbury, near St Albans in Hertfordshire, which remains a primary residential centre for Haringey's long-term mentally handicapped patients. Between them they have ensured that the 'mad' and the 'weak-minded' have remained hidden and forgotten by the rest of the population, including those who run the local health service.

Paradoxically, you can see Claybury from several miles away if you know where to look. The huge hundred-foot-high red-brick water tower, now a listed building, sticks up above the surrounding trees and buildings announcing the presence of one of those truly massive Victorian public institutions which are instantly recognisable as hospitals or prisons. It is on the edge of Epping Forest. Outside there is a village pond and executive-style homes which sell for upwards of £150,000. It is a highly desirable commuter dormitory beside London's green belt. Inside the hospital there are nearly 300 acres of trees, grass and scattered buildings which could be mistaken for an expensive public school or even a stately home in the Victorian style if they weren't so dog-eared and down at heel. Everything about Claybury is big, even massive. The administrative block sports high corridors, huge wood-panelled rooms and stained glass windows. It is linked to the forty or so wards by a reputed seven *miles* of corridor, much of it wide enough to drive a car down; veritable indoor streets used by the patients as places to meet, exchange information and, in the case of one where there is a 'boutique', to shop. At the end of these massive tentacles each ward is a self-contained world in itself; a complex of rooms with a dormitory, day room, bathrooms and administrative office where in the past upwards of fifty patients have lived, slept, eaten and passed most of their days, supplemented by occasional forays out into the rest of the hospital to work or socialise; big tall rooms, fifteen-foot and a hundred-foot long, with flourescent lighting, lino covered floors and well used furniture.

Much has changed in the hospital's ninety years, but it cannot so easily shake off its overbearing Victorian heritage. New drug treatments and changes in thinking about psychiatric health care have reduced the number of patients but it is hard to reduce the size of the buildings and those patients who remain rattle around the cavernous wards and corridors like lost souls.

Changes in psychiatric thinking have loosened up the style of the regime from a regimented, custodial operation to a style and approach more conducive to positively improving the mental well-being of its patients: more individuality; better personal relations between staff and patients; a greater emphasis on constructive creative activity. It is a brave and optimistic attempt to defy the inevitably de-humanising scale of the place. In such a setting old habits die hard and staff and outside support groups like the League of Friends, who should know better, are not immune from the old ways. Patients who have slept in the same bed, in the same place, in the same ward, for thirty years have a label on the end of the bed with their name; ditto their wardrobe, the bathroom, the kitchen and the toilets. 'I always wonder who they are for,' mused a relatively new nurse. 'They can't be for the patients; they know better than us where their bed is. They don't need to be told that the toilet is the toilet and where the kitchen is.' Recently the League of Friends donated a new TV set to this ward and sure enough some days later along came a workman and banged up a notice patronisingly inscribed 'Donated by the League of Friends'. 'Who wants to know? Who is it for, the patients, the visitors, the hospital inspectorate or the greater glory of the League of Friends?' asked the nurse.

After years of neglect, hospitals like this have become an NHS priority area. In the late 1960s and early 1970s a series of well-publicised scandals in long-stay hospitals drew attention to their plight. The *News of the World* carried a dramatic front page story of violence and cruelty at Ely psychiatric hospital near Cardiff in 1969, and a subsequent inquiry found an 'unduly casual attitude towards sudden death' among staff and 'an acceptance of old-fashioned, unduly rough and undesirably low standards of nursing care'. A year later there were similar allegations of violence and ill-treatment of mentally handicapped patients by staff at Farleigh hospital near Bristol. An inquiry revealed that the hospital's main buildings dated from 1838 and that the administrative office and medical consulting room were 'dismally and wholly inadequate'. It concluded that 'a grossly handicapped group of patients received far too little attention'. Three nurses were convicted of violence. Yet a third inquiry was set up to look into similar charges at Whittington hospital near Preston, one of the country's largest psychiatric institutions with over 20,000 beds, and others followed with unnerving monotony at South Ockenden and Normanton hospital for the mentally handicapped in Middlesex. The detailed recommendations varied, but almost without exception they emphasised the desperate need for more and better resources. As the Ely inquiry put it: 'the over-riding objectives . . . can only be achieved if substantially increased financial resources are made available'.[1] But their 'priority' status, although increasing their political and public profile, has failed to produce significant improvements in their material well-being, particularly on the long-stay back wards. In amongst the few wards which have been thoughtfully and carefully modernised at Claybury the majority remain neglected, drab and paint-chipped.

Money anyway cannot buy the necessary nursing staff which long-stay hospitals have always failed to recruit in sufficient numbers and staff levels are substantially worse than anything in the acute service. In its recruitment literature Claybury makes a valiant attempt to sound attractive. It emphasises that there is a bus terminal within the grounds and that 'all the facilities of central London' are only forty-five minutes away. But there is no escaping the fact that locked inside its acres of grounds, beyond the reach of the London underground train service, it is an isolated and inward-looking community with very little to offer the career-minded nurse or care worker. In 1985 the nursing budget was under-spent by some £40,000 because the hospital could not attract sufficient qualified staff. Some nurses believe this understates the true size of the problem because the budget has always underestimated the real needs of the hospital. But whatever the true picture, everybody agrees that the result is that hospitals like Claybury depend heavily on student nurses to make up the numbers. Even this does not guarantee all wards are adequately staffed twenty-four hours a day. Sometimes there is no night cover.

Much more seriously, about 50 per cent of Claybury's long-stay wards have been turned down by the English National Board for Nursing, Midwifery and Health Visiting, which is responsible for nurse training, as suitable training environments and staff numbers on these cannot be boosted by students. It means that for long periods of the day some wards can be down to one member of staff, a nursing level which has a crippling effect on the richness and variety of life available to patients. One nurse means that the administrative and basic nursing work takes over and there is nobody left to foster an active social or recreational programme, an essential ingredient where many people are largely incapable of generating any activity for themselves and left to their own devices sink into a vacant torpor. 'Normal' social interaction grinds to a standstill; outings to the local pub or shops become impossible; there is nobody to 'lead' a trip through the endless hospital corridors to the social club. Those who can, do so of their own accord, those who can't, don't. In such an environment new thinking about psychiatry makes very little impact, especially on the old back wards where some of the patients have lived for thirty, forty, even fifty years, products of the pre-war and war years, and are still firmly wedded to the dependent and debilitating habits of institutional living: up at 6 a.m., though for the last twenty years they have not had to get up until 8 a.m.; gobble down the food though today there is no pressure to get meals out of the way; and into bed at 8 p.m. although there is no longer a formal bed-time. Patients like this do not complain if their food is cold, as it sometimes is, and they do not even kick up a fuss if there is not enough of it and there often is not. They do not seem to expect anything else. Claybury remains, according to the hospital's nursing officer Malcolm Scott, 'an awful, appalling environment in which to practise psychiatry'. The regime may have become more enlightened and mental health may have become a priority, isolating hospitals like Claybury from the mainstream of NHS cuts, but the hospital service has neither the staff nor facilities to break free from the institutional and impoverished style of life which has always characterised it.

Few staff, nursing or administrative, have illusions about these shortcomings. Staff on Ward T2 at Claybury, a long-stay or continuing-care ward for men, know that one of the

biggest difficulties their patients face, perhaps the biggest, is
the legacy this regime has bequeathed them; whatever they
were originally admitted for, and the records are sometimes
vague and categories loose, has now been overlaid by years
of regimented life and institutionalisation has become a
disease in itself.

They are acutely aware of the drawbacks of large-scale
group living and its concomitant lack of privacy. Big
dormitories which remain dormitories no matter how
carefully they are partitioned with curtains and wardrobes,
double bathrooms, woefully inadequate storage facilities for
individual patients and a laundry system which not only
mangles new clothes in record time but virtually guarantees
that they get lost within a matter of weeks in a massive pile
of undifferentiated clothing, which is then arbitrarily distributed to the hospital as a whole. It is a form of collective
living which buries all but the psychologically most robust
and these are few and far between. One nurse recalled how
he had been left to look after four patients one day when the
rest of the ward had gone on an outing. The four – the most
timid, insecure and least able – had 'chosen' to stay at
'home'. But left alone on the ward they had begun to co-
operate and talk in ways they had never done before. 'I
became aware,' he recalls, 'how damaging large groups can
be for some people. They would do much better in a smaller
home.'

This is precisely what is now proposed. In 1983 the
Department of Health announced plans to close down the
large, long-stay hospitals and replace them with various
forms of community care, a holdall term for a network of
small and localised hostels and day centres. Claybury is to be
one of the first to go, an unwitting test-bed for the new
approach. Others in the area, which have also traditionally
taken people from Haringey, are to follow. It should be a
cause for celebration but as the date approaches many
people are not so sure.

The idea of community care goes back some years and subsequently became a cornerstone of the 1974–79 Labour government's policy towards what it designated the 'priority' groups. For people in long-stay hospitals the broad and guiding principle is that people should be maintained in their own homes where possible and failing this, in small 'people-centred' or open settings, which avoid the isolation and debilitating regimes of the big hospitals. Taken in this broad sense there are few disagreements.

But such a loose definition provides an uncertain guide to implementing these aspirations and in the intervening years the term has become 'virtually meaningless', as a House of Commons report put it.[2] Part of the problem lies in persistent attempts by governments to widen the definition to include non-statutory services, often in the name of value for money rather than well-researched evidence that they had something unique to offer. It started with the Labour government, which, while supporting the guiding principle behind community care, also began to equate it, at least in part, with a much greater input from voluntary and informal sources; in other words, care *in* the community also became care *by* the community. This thinking was taken a step further by the incoming Conservative government which in 1981 published its own version of the Priorities document, called *Care in Action*. In many respects it hardly differed from the Labour government's scenario: it reaffirmed the same groups of people as being in need of priority treatment; it emphasised the need to find low cost solutions and to carefully husband NHS resources and it re-affirmed the importance of making innovative use of non-statutory and voluntary groups to help. But a number of commentators have argued that on the last two points it took the argument a very important stage further. First it started from the now more realistic assumption that the Health Service was not going to get much growth money in the foreseeable future and therefore there would be no extra resources available from central government to fund the priority services. As one observer put it: there was a change in emphasis 'which marks a retreat by central government from its respon- sibilities in caring for dependent groups through the provi- sion of extra resources'.[3] In practice, previous governments had taken the same route, but without actually saying so or making a point of it.

If, however, there were to be no extra resources for the priority groups, but they were to remain a priority, it followed that resources would have to come from elsewhere and it is on this point that *Care in Action* took a second significant step beyond anything argued in the Priorities document. *Care in Action* proposed, as one of its principal recommendations, that there should be a greater use of the informal, voluntary and, most significantly, private sectors in developing the caring services. Patrick Jenkin, the then Conservative health minister, made it abundantly clear in a speech during this period, just how much greater this use should be when he affirmed that the government was now assuming that the informal and voluntary sectors would become the main providers of care for dependent people: 'We cannot operate as if the state services are central providers with a few volunteers here and there to back them up. Instead we should recognise that the informal sector lies at the centre with state services and the voluntary sector providing expertise and support.'

This indeed was a new emphasis. Jenkin's thinking may have been influenced by a report on voluntary and informal carers known as the Wolfenden Report.[4] This examined the way in which dependent people had always been cared for by a variety of agencies which formed, in effect, what it called picturesquely a 'mixed economy' of welfare, in which state services were complemented by the voluntary and private sectors. This was an idea close to the heart of Jenkin's thinking and whether directly or indirectly influenced by it, he enthusiastically pursued the logic, explaining to health authorities that they should no longer expect to fund the priority services exclusively on their own and that they should look for support from, and ways of co-operating with, private and voluntary groups. Many have been unhappy with this broader definition, and as one observer wrote,

It is hard to escape the conclusion that this latest consultative document, while continuing to mouth the rhetoric of meeting the needs of dependent groups, has seized upon community care in conjunction with the Wolfenden report concept of the mixed economy of welfare, to reduce the 'burden' of care on the state. The emphasis is no longer focused on the importane of meeting the needs of dependent groups of people for humanitarian reasons but on the economic imperative to reduce state expenditure.[5]

The all-party House of Commons Social Services Select Committee also looked at community care and profoundly disagreed with what it saw as an attempt to dilute the role of the statutory services.[6] It wrote that community care should not be used as a catch-phrase to cover:

* Saving money by getting people out of hospital;
* Care by families and volunteers rather than state care;
* The transfer of responsibility from health authorities to social service departments.

Instead it *should* imply:

* A preference for 'home-life' over institutional care;
* The pursuit of the ideal of normalisation and integration and the avoidance, so far as possible, of separate provision, segregation and restriction;
* Small over large;
* Local over distant.

In sum, 'appropriate care should be provided for individuals in such a way as to enable them to lead as normal an existence as possible given their particular disabilities'.

Even this apparently straightforward assertion is, in fact, no more than a re-emphasis of the broad principles, rather than a serious attempt to translate them into something which can be planned, budgeted and built. The reality is that despite a decade of talking about it, community care has never been taken seriously, perhaps until now. It does not exist as a comprehensive range of services anywhere in Britain and we are therefore profoundly ignorant about what it could be and how it might work. Alan Maynard and Nick Bosanquet of the Centre for Health Economics at York University have written in a recent paper commissioned by a group of health service professional associations, that whilst community care programmes for the elderly, mentally ill and mentally handicapped are 'developing as a result of their own internal incentives and the impact of outside influences, it is quite clear that the evolution of care practices for these groups . . . [is] . . . not informed by knowledge about the costs and effects'.[7] They maintain that there is a 'lamentable absence of evidence' about relative costs of institutional care and an equal lack of evidence about its relative effectiveness.

The policy is consequently being implemented largely in the dark and there are important areas of discussion going by default about the gross quantity of provision needed, whether it is appropriate for all dependent people in all circumstances, what forms it should take and how much it will cost. The difficulty with discussions about quantity of care is that nobody knows where the base line is. While governments have tended to emphasise the idea of a straightforward switch in provision from institutions to the community – with the implied assumption that it is a straightforward exchange of patients from one kind of care to another – the reality is that the Health Service starts from the position of an enormous and uncharted backlog of need which has led some commentators to talk of an already existing 'crisis' in community care. 'The almost obsessive concentration in public policy on the mechanism for "getting people out of hospital" has sometimes obscured the basic fact that *most mentally ill and handicapped people already live in the community* whether with their families, in lodgings, group homes, hostels or private accommodation,' wrote the Commons select committee. 'This concern for people in hospital has tended to obscure . . . an approaching *crisis in the community*.'[8]

Nobody knows the dimensions of this 'crisis'. The nature, if not the size, of it, however, was dramatically highlighted in 1984 by *The Sunday Times*. It started with a letter from a Southampton reader who wrote, 'The reality of community care for very many sick and disturbed individuals is nothing more than a Dickensian life-style. They are taken out of a nineteenth century institution and put into twentieth century poverty.' In the wake of this missive the paper's social services correspondent, Marjorie Wallace, went to Southampton to see for herself, explaining that the city was generally considered to have a good reputation for social service provision among local authorities. She found, in her own words, 'thousands of mentally ill people . . . abandoned in squalid lodging houses or even simply decanted onto the streets'. She goes on:

I found Nick Rayment, a thirty-seven year old schizophrenic, lying pale and shaking in a Southampton bed and breakfast house. It was nine o'clock on a bleak autumn morning. He had been lying in his bed for two days, nursing bottles of Valium and penicillin, listening to 'the voices' in his head, too afraid to move out. 'I'm dying,' he said. 'I need help'. Ron Scott, at the St James's Night Shelter, talked about Terry – a 'pitiful man' with the mentality of a twelve year old. 'The hospital wouldn't have him because he was not treatable. He got badly beaten up on the streets. In the end we had to advise him to go shoplifting so that he could get into a police station. It was the only thing to do'.[9]

The reality, if not the lurid details, of this account were underlined in the same year by a much more sober document from the Richmond Fellowship, an organisation which runs a series of therapeutic half-way homes for mentally ill people. It reported that it believed the mental health system was being run down in the name of community care but 'an alternative system is not being built up at anything like an equivalent rate'. It claimed that some 143,000 hospital places had been lost since 1954.

But government spokesmen have been unable to show that the necessary alternative services have been provided . . . the wide range of substitute provision – hostels, group homes, subsidised housing, domiciliary supervisors, day centres, sheltered workshops – has not been established on an adequate scale. It was admitted by the government spokesman . . . that only about half the number of places in non-hospital residential units, only about one third of the day hospital places and only about a quarter of the places in local authority and voluntary day centres recommended in the government white paper of 1975 were actually available. There are parallel deficits in staffing ratios.[10]

More recently, Dr Malcolm Weller, a consultant psychiatrist at Friern Barnet hospital, is one of a number of commentators who have observed an apparent correlation between the fall in hospital populations and an increase in the prison population, with a particularly marked rise in what Weller calls 'psycho-pathology' among prisoners, to a level which is significantly higher than the average for the population as a whole. 'It's only a correlation, not an indication of causal relation, but the higher rate of psychiatric morbidity in prisons makes . . . a compelling reason to doubt the success of community policies,' he writes.[11] He points out that with some thirty mental hospitals closing over the current decade and fourteen new prisons opening, the trend may well get worse.

The House of Commons Social Services Select Committee was quite explicit about the issue:

Although community care has only attracted wide-spread public attention comparatively recently, the process of running down mental illness hospitals has been quietly proceeding for decades and for at least the last ten years in the case of mental handicap hospitals. We are now at a crucial stage; there is ample evidence of the decanting of patients . . . in years past without sufficient development of services for them. This has produced a proportion of chronically ill and mentally handicapped people with nowhere to go . . . *the stage has now been reached where the rhetoric of community care has to be matched by action*. If the present uneven balance of concern is not redressed, all energies will be bent on providing services for people coming out of hospital, only to find equal pressure to use these facilities coming from people not currently in hospital.[12]

The logical consequence is that this untapped demand will swamp the new provision aimed primarily at those now coming out of hospital and that neither group will be adequately catered for.

A different but equally important area of debate involves the appropriateness of community care for all dependent people. DHSS pronouncements appear to treat rather lightly the fact that a place like Claybury houses hundreds of people who have spent major periods – perhaps the major period – of their lives in hospital and for whom it is the nearest thing they have to a home. Many are in their late sixties and seventies and in the normal course of events would only leave when they die. Nobody knows whether or not these people will ever be sufficiently rehabilitated to make community care a feasible option for them and the worry is that if they are forced out in the name of community care, it will be at a terrible cost to their fragile and confused sense of stability.

To get an impression of the scale of the problem I spent a little time on Ward T2, home for twenty-eight 'medium dependency' men who range in age from their early fifties to their late seventies and who have lived in Claybury for between twenty and fifty years. It is reckoned by staff to house some of the hospital's most capable long-term residents; if they cannot be helped and encouraged to make a success of moving out of the hospital into smaller 'community' units, other long-term patients have got a very slim chance indeed. But recently one of its most able patients, a man in his mid sixties who has lived at Claybury for at least twenty-five years, was moved to a smaller rehabilitation ward with an eye to transferring him to a community home in the near future, and it has proved much less straightforward than anybody suspected. Rehabilitation is a fairly gentle business. It involves teaching patients basic social skills like how to use a knife and fork or drink from a cup without spilling too much, personal hygiene and perhaps a little cooking and washing. But Jim has found the *thought* of change traumatic. He has had several changes in his drug treatment, although before the move he was regarded by staff as extremely stable, and he has developed new mannerisms and twitches. He used to be an enthusiastic stamp collector and ran a stamp business on the ward, buying and selling for other patients. All this has gone, at least for the time being, and when he returns to T2 to visit friends, staff watch him with anxiety and misgivings; if they cannot rehabilitate Jim, they believe they have got very little chance with the rest.

Patients on T2 know all about the impending change; it's a regular topic of conversation at the weekly ward meetings between staff and patients and some claim they are looking forward to it; they are looking forward to what they believe will be more freedom and better facilities. But it is hard to know whether they really understand what it is all about. One told me he hated Claybury and would prefer to go back to Broadmoor where he had come from; failing that he would settle for what he called a group home. Another said he thought it would give him more opportunity to go down to the pub, though there is a pub almost outside the gates of Claybury which he is free to go to. A third told me he could not remember how long he had lived at Claybury, but so long as he did not have to live alone in the community, he believed he would get along just fine. Only one patient admitted he was apprehensive. He has lived at Claybury a very long time – staff said forty-five years – and has, as far as is possible, become part of the fabric of the hospital. He knows in detail the staff he comes into contact with; how many children they have and what colour their car is. If somebody is on holiday or off sick he is keen to know whether they are all right. He works in the garden with a fellow patient he has known for forty years. He did not say he did not want to go to a group home so much as imply that the thought deeply distressed him. But it is hard to know how to judge these statements. Perhaps they should be taken at face value, but it would be naive not to allow for the fact that patients at Claybury, particularly old hands, live in some dread of authority and it is quite possible that talking to a complete stranger who is introduced to them by a nurse, they will give the answer they believe is wanted. Certainly the nurses I talked to, even those fully committed to community care, believe that most of Claybury's long-term patients dread the change.

Peter, a senior nurse on T2, is one of them. He believes the kindest thing would be to allow the hospital's existing long-term population to quietly live out their remaining days in a familiar environment. 'I cannot believe it's the best thing for these people,' he says, looking round at the ten or so patients sitting around him in the common room of T2. 'The best thing would be to give them decent facilities here. Some of them are going to die in the next five or ten years anyway; what a way to spend the last years of your life worrying about where you are going to live.'

My conviction is that this *is* their home, I'm just passing through and my job is to make their life as enjoyable as I can. I know other nurses have different points of view. They are committed to a more rehabilitative role, a more clear-cut patient/nurse division; they assume that Claybury is a temporary stopping place for patients and the important thing is that they can move on. I don't agree because I don't think that many patients want to. It's a different way of looking at people and at the job. I suppose there are different assumptions about what is possible.

Others share his misgivings. Malcolm Weller has recorded very similar concerns. He has written: 'Following hospital discharge there is a high risk of suicide, estimated among schizophrenics to be 17 times that expected of the population as a whole [and] violent crimes are committed 22.5 times more often by schizophrenic patients.'[13] He reports problems of 'destitution, disease and death' among recently discharged psychiatric patients. Faced with evidence like this there is a growing body of opinion which believes that society, having grossly mishandled these people's lives in the past, owes them a quiet and dignified old age in the places they have now called home.

Moreover, it is by no means certain that every psychiatric patient, even in the enlightened, post-Claybury, era, when problems of institutionalisation are a thing of the past, will be able to cope with the loose network of hostels and day centres that will make up community provision. Nor, for that matter, that the public will be able to cope with the more confused or disturbed patients. 'Informed opinion is slowly returning to the idea that there will always be a substantial number of mentally dependent people who are entitled to some sort of protection and support which may involve their partial withdrawal from the rest of the community,' wrote the House of Commons Social Services Select Committee in a 1985 report.[14] Malcolm Weller, in the same letter referred to above, points out that the enthusiasm for day centres presupposes that 'apathetic, avolitional, schizophrenic patients will attend on a regular basis, rather than spending their days in bed in the conglomerate of bed-sitters managed by "caring landladies" '.

Like so much else in this area we simply do not know. In the past decade the inpatient population of mental illness hospitals has dropped from almost 100,000 in the early 1970s to around 69,000 in the mid-1980s. But research into what has happened to these thousands of people has hardly begun. 'It is truly remarkable,' wrote the *British Medical Journal*, 'that we do not know what proportion have settled successfully in the community with family or other support groups, have struggled on in a lonely abyss, have lived a life of destitution or have given up and returned to hospital.'[15]

Many psychiatric staff believe that even if their patients were ready to face society, society is not ready to receive them. They know that they and their patients are isolated and that part of the reason for this is that society has chosen that it should be this way. They have experienced at first hand public indifference and hostility to the odd and unusual and they have no confidence that the 'community' cares at all.

'In a hospital you can shout, or cry or laugh out loud and nobody bothers. You try doing that while you're sitting on the top deck of a bus travelling from your hostel or B&B to your day centre,' one nurse told me. 'Mannerisms which seem odd to an "ordinary person" are accepted as normal in a psychiatric hospital. I don't believe the public is tolerant of even our best-behaved patients. I have taken small groups into pubs without number which have turned round and asked us to leave. Do you expect them to accept our more disturbed cases?' The difficulty of making out a case for a continuation of some form of asylum is that it allows us, the general public, to persist in our bigoted and intolerant view of people who do not meet our perceived standards of conduct. But this said, there may be instances in which certain individuals and society would benefit from some kind of limited asylum option. We have to be realistic about what society will tolerate in people's behaviour and about the pressures this in turn puts on some individuals. The trap is in assuming that past forms of asylum are the only forms it can take; it does not have to mean the large, impoverished and impersonal institutions we have currently made it.

The third area of uncertainty concerns the costs of the whole operation, an issue of critical importance when budgets have become so tight. Circulars from the DHSS have been oddly misleading and unhelpful in the past. The Conservative government's *Care in Action* report[16] looked at the relative costs of institutional and community care and adopted a somewhat cautious approach to the relative cost benefits of the latter.

It discussed a DHSS study into community care which, it said, took the view that 'community care is not necessarily cheaper than care in an institution'. It went on, 'As is well known, the scale of support that some people require if they are to live at home is considerable,' and in an appendix it emphasised that 'few studies have compared *both* the cost *and* the effect of different patterns of care,' and went on to add that much research is needed in this area although it would be a 'mistake to underestimate the methodological difficulties'. But five months later the department released a second consultative report called *Care in the Community*[17] which took an altogether more optimistic view of the community care picture. 'Although the cost to the community health and personal social services of providing care for people transferred from hospital is difficult to assess, there are good reasons for believing that in many cases it would be both lower and better value.' It did not elaborate on where the 'good reasons' came from or whether the previous 'methodological difficulties' had been overcome, and we are still waiting for a clear elaboration of this issue, but it effectively formed the basis of what has become official Conservative orthodoxy.

It is almost certainly nonsense; few people now believe that community care, unless it involves a substantial input from voluntary and informal sources, is cheaper than hospital provision and many believe it will be more expensive. Nevertheless, as a result of uncertainties about the numbers of people who will need it and the cost of providing it, budgets are being proposed which place a huge doubt over the viability of the entire project and it is extremely improbable, on the basis of the money being offered to health authorities, that a comprehensive community programme can be established in the foreseeable future. The difficulty for local health authorities is that faced with the apparent unreality of DHSS statements and a lack of hard information about what is needed and how much it will cost, they are being forced to piece together a strategy with very uncertain parameters and which may turn out to be unrealisable.

The Local Story

Haringey health district has little more than the haziest of ideas of how many people its new community programme should be catering for, but it is possible to piece together a rough and ready estimate. It is known that there are several hundred too few hospital beds for geriatric patients and that this has caused residential homes and sheltered housing run by the local authority social services department to silt up. Residential homes are accommodating people who should be in hospital, sheltered houses contain people who should be in a home and the domiciliary services like district nurses and home helps are struggling to support people at home who should be in both. The health authority is building new ward blocks for geriatrics which should be ready in the late 1980s, but even then it will be nearly a hundred beds short of the level recommended by the DHSS for the size of the local population. It is hoping to make up for this with increased community services so that people like Eileen Thomas can escape the revolving door of hospital and home that they are now trapped in. On top of this there are probably several thousand families who, since the early 1970s, have been encouraged to look after their mentally handicapped children at home. Most have welcomed this shift in policy, but as parents and children grow older the policy has begun to break down. A combination of elderly parents and demanding adolescents is no longer viable and dozens of families are known to be on the verge of breaking up under the strain. There is a pressing need to provide something else for this first generation of home-reared, post-1970s mentally handicapped adolescents.

In addition there is an unrecorded number of mentally ill or disturbed people who, up until recently, would have disappeared onto the back wards of a mental hospital for the rest of their lives, but, in the name of enlightened psychiatry, have been discharged into the 'community' and told to fend for themselves. The average length of stay in a psychiatric hospital today is around seventeen days, which means that in the case of most psychiatric patients, family and friendship networks are still intact and they can return from whence they came like any other hospital patient. The vast numbers who disappeared into psychiatric hospitals in the past, gradually succumbing to the depredations of institutionalisation, no longer exist. But there are some who are so confused or disruptive – usually they are loosely categorised as schizophrenic – that they can never be successfully returned to their homes and it is this group which is part of today's problem. Many are believed to be eking out profoundly unsatisfactory lives in hostels or bed and breakfasts financed by social security payments. Most are not so self-evidently dramatic as *The Sunday Times* examples, but a small survey of chronic psychiatric patients discharged from Claybury found that the majority were living in sub-standard accommodation at an appalling standard of living with very little support from the statutory services and with poor social contacts with the rest of society. There could be as many as a couple of hundred in the Haringey area at the moment.

A further group of mentally disturbed people, crying out for attention, are the elderly mentally infirm who fit into neither of the conventional mental health or elderly categories of accommodation. They are drawn from two distinct groups: those over sixty-five who are succumbing to senile dementia for the first time and those over sixty-five who have been mentally ill all their lives and are due to be decanted from the psychiatric hospitals. Both need facilities, but it is the first which is an uncharted number. Nobody knows how many are living at home or have been siphoned off into the private sector because there is nowhere else for them to go. 'We don't know where to put them but there are an awful lot who should be getting care because they are a danger to themselves,' I was told by a senior health authority administrator. 'Everybody opts out. The GP opts out because he knows he cannot find Mrs Jones a place. I have a sense of a bubbling mass of humanity living on the edge of sanity and safety and every now and then one of them falls off and we hear about it.' Liz Morris, an organiser for Haringey Old People's Welfare, is blunter: 'Dementia is the in-thing to stay at home with. People are coping with tremendous problems of mental confusion at home; it's horrific. What we are seeing is that the psychiatric service is copping out by saying "yes that person should have a bed, but we haven't got any".' The health authority recognises the problem and is committed to opening a number of wards and day centres catering specially for them but it expects this programme, which is anyway still mostly on paper, to fall short of the relatively arbitrary DHSS norm by at least a hundred places. These people will remain the responsibility of the community programme.

One group with an intimate awareness of the scale of the 'community crisis' and the deluge of demand which may be just round the corner, is the small and precariously funded Haringey care attendant scheme, which provides back-up for people caring for a relative or friend. It has no idea how many 'informal carers', as they are known, there are in the district, but it is aware that its service is only scratching the surface of the need. A crude rule of thumb suggests there could be as many as several thousand carers who are in various stages of buckling under the strain of being full-time, unpaid, nursemaids. People like JT who took early retirement after his mother, a woman in her 80s was found to be suffering from Alzheimers disease, the most common form of senile dementia. She needs constant attention, twenty-four hours a day, seven days a week. She has to be physically helped to get up, to dress, go to the toilet and eat. Frequently she wakes up several times a night. JT gets two afternoons off a week thanks to the care attendant scheme but he needs more if he is to live any kind of decent life. There is no help during the night, at weekends or for holidays and JT, who was at breaking point before he got help from the scheme, is still barely coping. If, or perhaps when, he does, his mother will need a great deal more than a part-time care attendant. The scheme meanwhile is only able to help fifty other people like him, although it knows of twice that number who need help. That still leaves upwards of 2,000 who could and should be able to turn to the community services for help and might do so any day.

Not all of this unmet demand is the sole responsibility of the National Health Service. Community care, as a concept, is predicated on close liaison and co-operation between the NHS and local authority social service departments which are responsible for those areas of care which do not require more than a minimal medical input. This includes residential and day care facilities for all the priority groups. But national surveys have suggested that local authorities have their own problems in meeting this commitment. The Campaign for the Mentally Handicapped, in a survey in the early 1980s, found that economic restraint had 'virtually stopped' local authority spending on new residential accommodation for the mentally handicapped and that the 'rate of increase in hostel places over the next few years can be expected to drop sharply'. 'There have been profound problems with competing resources and priorities,' it wrote.[18]

These findings were virtually duplicated by a review of local government spending on services for the mentally handicapped by the *Guardian*'s former social service correspondent David Hencke, who reviewed eighteen reports by the National Development Team for the Mentally Handicapped covering areas from London to North Yorkshire.[19] 'In nearly every area the strategy [of community care] appears to have failed. One main reason . . . is lack of cash in nearly every department to take responsibility for people leaving hospital.' Another study found that one quarter of local authorities provide no day care at all for the mentally ill and one fifth provide no residential accommodation.

Haringey borough council is not one of them. For nearly twenty years it has been a relatively left-wing Labour local authority firmly wedded to maintaining and even expanding, where possible, public services, and the social service department is generally considered to be doing a good job. Indeed several people in the health authority remarked on it. But it has had its budget clipped by rate capping and it cannot provide all the services it would like to.

To help elderly and physically disabled people live independent lives at home it provides a range of home aids and adaptations designed to make life easier, anything from a wheelchair lift to a potato peeler. But the aids and adaptations service is chronically short of money and there is a long waiting list for attention. 'It's this week's joke,' according to Liz Morris, who claims people are being told they may have to wait up to twelve months for an assessment of their need. 'It has got worse and worse over the last three years; it's slowly improving now, but there is a tremendous bottleneck . . . People are dying before they can get their aids; sometimes the service appears to simply run out of money.'

One of the cores of domiciliary provision is the home help service which supports a large number of, usually, elderly people who would not otherwise to able to live at home. It is a good 'value for money' service, but unless it gets more resources it cannot cope with the increasing number of severely dependent people who both want, and are obliged, to live at home. Jean Smith, a home help organiser, dreams of what she calls a 'proper care service' for these people. As she says,

My idea would go like this: early in the morning, start the day, a cup of tea, helping the client get up, especially if they are in a wet bed; lunch time, check they have had a lunch from meals on wheels and that they have eaten at least some of it; four or five o'clock, check they have had some supper or a snack, and then again at eight or nine, ten o'clock at night you need someone to help put the person to bed if they are not able to do it themselves. I don't think you can be talking about anything less than that if you are talking about good community care.

In reality the pattern is more likely to be one home help visit in the morning to make the bed, change the sheets if they are wet, organise breakfast and do the housework and shopping, meals on wheels at lunch time and a sandwich and flask of tea that the home help has prepared, for tea. If the person is severely dependent he or she will be got up and put to bed by a district nurse. But the district nursing service has many calls on its time and nurses cannot guarantee when they will make a visit. Evenings can be a particularly humiliating experience. Depending on the work load, bed time can be at any time during the evening shift, which means in practice between 6 p.m. and 10 p.m., too early if you are at the beginning of the shift, too late if you are at the end. 'I have been to visit people in the summer, sun streaming down outside, kids playing and they are in bed and it's only six o'clock,' a health visitor told me. 'It's not even evening, it's late afternoon and somehow they are in bed. That doesn't help clients who are confused. What happens if they want to watch "Crossroads", every night; who gets up and turns it off if they haven't got remote control which most of them cannot afford? They haven't even got some of the very basic things we take for granted.'

There is also a danger that, under pressure, community staff create a relationship with their 'clients' or 'patients' which is almost as debilitatingly dependent and institutional as any relationship in a long-stay hospital. 'It's so easy to go in and take over, isn't it; get them up quick, get them dressed.' Jean Smith continued:

It's not 'OK, here is the bowl, you have a wash while I clean and then I'll wash your back or feet and then I'll put your vest on and you can put on the shirt.' It's 'come on let's get you up, it's cold in here and we'll get you sat in a chair and I'll make your breakfast.' It's taking over so that the client isn't even trying to retain some things for themselves. If somebody had an hour-and-a-half they could well do it properly, but not in the time we have got. The temptation is to do it all for them as fast as you can, instead of helping and supporting them so that they can do more for themselves; you do it for them.

The social service department is outspokenly critical of what it perceives as the burden it is being forced to carry as a result of shortcomings in the district health service. 'The goal of providing adequate community care to allow old people to remain in their own homes is a long way off in Haringey,' it has written. 'This is because the GP/primary care service and the vital district nursing service, is under-staffed, under-developed and under-funded.' It might have added that, as Haringey's population follows the national trend and there is a gradual increase in the dependent population of elderly and handicapped people, there will be an increase in demand on the Health Service and these failings will become more acute.

What renders the whole thing somewhat farcical is that Haringey health district has virtually no funds with which to meet this enormous and burgeoning demand. In RAWP-losing districts there is no new or extra money to finance new services and everything will have to come out of cuts or rationalisations in the existing programme. The district reckons it needs at least £200,000 a year on top of the existing community budget to generally improve community medical services and fund improvements aimed specifically at the elderly. This will have to come from savings made in the acute hospital sector, though as we have seen before there could be problems in matching savings to services.

What it cannot find from its own resources is cash for the mentally ill and handicapped. This is intended to come from the closure of the long-stay hospitals through what is known as the 'dowry' system. Each patient discharged from a long-stay hospital brings with him or her a 'dowry' which is supposed to fund an alternative community place. Thus hospitals losing patients lose money and districts receiving them gain on a one to one basis. In fact it is not quite so simple because a district needs to construct a community facility before patients can leave hospital and regional health authorities have accepted that there will need to be a period of double funding during which they will have to pay for both. Indeed it will never be a straight cash exchange because, as we have also seen before, marginal and average costs are not the same and just as you cannot close an acute specialty and expect to save the entire cost of running it, so you cannot discharge a patient from a long-stay hospital and expect to save the entire cost of that patient. Each patient's funding contributes to the overall fixed running costs of an establishment and the more you reduce the patients, the higher the fixed running costs per remaining patient become. Regional health authorities will therefore have to provide both dowries for outgoing patients and increased funding for those remaining.

What the procedure completely fails to do, however, is to provide any funding for those thousands of mentally ill and handicapped people who are not in a hospital. In effect, districts are being expected to fund two groups of people from cash resources designed to be sufficient for one. This only makes sense if community care is roughly half the price of its institutional equivalent, and we have seen that there is no evidence to suggest that this is the case. Haringey health district faces a difficult and painful series of stark choices. Either it can cater for those coming out of hospital with their dowries and ignore the pressing needs of those already in the community, or it can concentrate on the needs of those currently living under pressure at home and slow down its reception of people from the hospitals. The trouble with this option is that hospital discharges are the only source of funding. It could go for a mixture of the two, but the risk is of trying to spread resources so thinly that nobody is adequately provided for. Finally, it can try and drum up some of the shortfall from the private or voluntary sectors, in line with the government's 'mixed economy' of welfare. It is an absurd dilemma. Among those I talked to, the privately-favoured solution is a version of number two and four. 'You have got to turn off the taps before you can empty the bath,' was how it was put to me. The aspiration would be to provide improved facilities to allow a gradual, but much slower decanting so that those already living in the community are the first to benefit. It is a choice which, because it cannot rely on dowry money, depends on the voluntary sector being able to meet some of the shortfall – in Haringey a safe, if morally questionable assumption.

The drawback is that it will prolong the agony of the long-stay hospitals. Morale in these is already low and what is crushing any latent idealism there may be among staff for a new beginning is a sense that the whole closure programme is not only out of their own control, but also out of control generally. From their point of view, projects come and go and dates alter in a random and arbitrary fashion which seems perverse and insulting. Nurses at Claybury have lost count of the number of visits they have had from authorities about to open a new community facility which subsequently sinks into oblivion, or of the plans they have been asked to draw up which never get further than the paper they are written on. One nurse recalled bitterly his experience several years ago when he was invited to join a group from the hospital which met weekly to discuss setting up a community home in the neighbourhood; their job was to decide what kind of facilities it should have and how it should be run. They got excited and involved, wrote up their ideas, passed them on to the authority and that was the last they heard of it for nine months. When it finally re-emerged most of their thinking had been thrown out as impractical or too expensive because over the planning period the hostel's budget had been cut in half. Uncertainty about the future, what is more, puts them in a difficult position in relation to their patients. Peter, a nurse on T2, told me,

The plans chop and change all the time. It's in the air that we will be the first long-stay ward to close. But whether that means distributing the patients elsewhere in the hospital or whether they will go outside, we don't know. The patients know that changes are in the air; we try to keep them informed, but we are not that clear ourselves.

Nor, against this background, are they clear about their own futures; how long they will have a job at the hospital for and what the alternatives might be. They do not like the sense of being out of control of their own destinies and many are dreaming of early retirement or looking for work elsewhere in a completely different field. Others are sitting it out with a deep sense of resigned inevitability, weary of the turbulence and uncertainty. 'I'm not afraid of the future, but I'm not over the moon about it. I don't really know what it will mean; what alterations there will be. I'm not exactly opposed to it and I'm certainly not apathetic about it, but I am profoundly cynical,' Peter told me.

In these circumstances it is not hard to envisage a scenario in which the hospitals literally die on their feet as the closure programme grinds on indefinitely and they are left with the most confused and difficult patients, declining budgets, falling morale and decaying buildings. What they need, as a minimum, is a clear and finite closure programme that they can work towards in a planned and orderly fashion. There is in this a clear clash of interests between districts aware of the demands of existing dependent people in their communities and hospitals aware of the pressures that the closure programme is putting on them. What is wrong in all this is that anybody should have to choose between one or the other and that the closure programmes should be so near to being botched.

It raises the question of how serious the government is about its community care programme and whether or not it is aware of the choices it is expecting local authorities to make. One way or another the government seems to be implying that it is prepared to live with the fact that thousands of mentally ill and handicapped people are going to have to put up with conditions which are generally agreed to be unsatisfactory for years to come. The only question is which group of people is going to bear the brunt of this suffering.

One potential source of funding, designed to encourage co-operation between the NHS and local authority social service departments, is called joint finance or joint funding and was launched by the Department of Health in the mid-1970s, at the beginning of the community care programme, when it was realised that most local authorities had neither the money nor the desire to contribute towards the community programme. The problem for the DHSS was that it had no power to force local authorities, who run their own social service departments, to prioritise social service spending and many had such poor provision that even with the best will in the world they would have found it impossible to finance the scale of the improvements needed out of their own resources. Many had virtually no provision at all. The joint funding scheme provided an incentive by offering them cash to improve their social service provision. It was specifically earmarked for projects which would keep people out of hospital and worked on the basis of local health authorities funding local authority projects for a given number of years, the finance gradually tapering off after five, seven or eleven years, as the local authority took up the strain.

Unfortunately, despite its relative priority, the funds have become increasingly tight. On paper it has grown rapidly since its introduction in 1975–76, when the annual national budget was £7 million. In 1985–86 it was £110 million. But much of this growth was in the 1970s when the annual budget doubled for a number of years. In recent years it has not kept pace with inflation and at district health authority level it is still very small indeed: £½ million in the case of Haringey in 1985–86. Even this figure is slightly deceptive because a number of projects tie up money over several years so that the amount of free or new funds available in any one year to distribute to new projects is small: £100,000 in the case of Haringey in 1985–86. In fact it is still smaller as Haringey health authority's budget is so tight that it has begun to fund its own projects from joint finance, projects which should really come out of the mainstream health budget. In 1985 it skimmed £20,000 to fund two extra health visitors, and in doing so nearly precipitated the collapse of, among other projects, Haringey's care attendant scheme (which was temporarily rescued by the social service department). This said, it has had an important effect at a local level in increasing co-operation between the health and social services. 'It is the only way we have of putting bricks on the bridges we might like to build between the two services,' is how Haringey's director of social services, David Townsend, put it. 'It is a bridge between services which have always got along uneasily. It's a bridge which creates a forum for them to get together and talk.' What it is not and never has been is a large enough source of funds to offset the other pressures on local authority resources and, as a result, many local authorities have, as we have seen, chosen or been forced to cut back on the so-called 'priority' areas.

It is worth recording in passing, that many worthwhile and costly initiatives may flounder because of cuts in a completely different areas of the National Health Service. The conglomerate of facilities which go to make up community care depend on being able to pick up people from home and transport them from one facility to another. Some of this transportation depends on the ambulance service. But the London ambulance service faces a falling budget until the mid-1990s and has been forced to reduce non-emergency transport, virtually halting services for people who are physically able to walk. Day centres, already underused because people cannot get to them, may have to be run below their capacity.

For community care to become a reality and for the shift from hospital and institutional care to the community to happen, various parts of a jigsaw need to come together. The policy requires unprecedented co-operation between health authorities, family practitioner committees and local authorities, and it requires each of these to meet their individual commitment to the new pattern of care. Today, many of the bits are still missing. The health authority is falling down on its commitments to community and primary health care and is unlikely to be able to fund the hostel, residential and day care facilities needed to make the shift from institutions a reality. The family practitioner committee is unable to exert any significant influence over GPs who will need to compensate for the rationalisation of the acute and long-stay hospitals and the local authority cannot afford to fund the levels of provision it considers necessary.

There are fears that the lack of funds is pervading and souring the whole approach to community care. 'One becomes so depressed and frustrated,' said one wheelchair-bound member of the Haringey Disablement Association. 'They just don't seem to know where they are going. They don't seem to be able to get their act together and I have lost confidence that they are going in the right direction. I don't believe any longer that they are going to do it properly.' She is particularly distressed by plans for residential homes, hostels and sheltered houses which, in her view, show signs of becoming 'mini-institutions', and she was outraged and horrified to overhear planners discussing the idea of increasing the 'productivity' of sheltered housing. 'They were talking about what happens when somebody from a sheltered home goes into hospital and they actually suggested moving somebody else in while the original inhabitant was in hospital; moving a stranger into your house! How can they even dream of such a thing? Are they talking about homes or are they talking about institutions? I despair.'

She is not alone. The House of Commons Social Services Select Committee summed up its findings in 1985 as follows:

None of those who submitted evidence to us were opposed to the basic principle of community care; but we have heard a chorus of deeply felt anxieties, protests and fears. The families of mentally handicapped and mentally ill people, those who currently and for the foreseeable future bear the brunt of care . . . have been the most expressive, both in criticism of the inadequacy of present levels of service and in their sceptical attitude towards the long-term trend away from hospital care. Many parents anxious to avert hospital admission for their children are sceptical as to the adequacy or sufficiency of the alternative arrangements. The caring profession . . . supports the thrust, but implementation to date is not satisfactory and immediate prospects are not bright . . . *there is a general and growing groundswell of opinion which is questioning the way in which so-called community care policies are operating in practice.*[20]

In their day the mental hospitals represented a major financial investment in staff and buildings to the Victorian ideal of good mental health care. Today that ideal has become grotesque and we are rightly pulling it down but we are not putting the same investment into replacing it. Britain is not a good place to be old or dependent unless you have got private means.

CHAPTER SIX

Past Caring

When Stan Field came home last week there was quite a reception committee waiting for him. The ambulance had bumped over the 'sleeping policemen' into the courtyard of the block of flats where he lives and deposited him at the bottom of his stairwell, next to a burnt-out car, partially disguised by a recent fall of snow. He had cautiously eased himself out of the vehicle and, with an ambulance attendant on each arm, painfully made his way up to his first floor flat. There he had been greeted by a district nurse, a home help from the social service department and his next-door neighbour, all alerted to the fact that after a week in hospital with an attack of bronchitis Stan was coming home to convalesce. Aged eighty-four and living alone, he was going to need some help.

It is a scene which has become increasingly common. As hospitals have stepped up the speed at which patients pass through them, the NHS has placed a growing reliance on the community services and informal networks of friends, to make up the difference. The scale of the shift is vividly illustrated in some of the hospital performance figures. The average length of stay has dropped from 9.4 days in 1978 to 7.8 days in 1984 and the figure is continuing to go on down.[1] More people than ever before are being treated on an outpatient or day patient basis. In the first half of the 1980s, spending on inpatient treatment rose 1.5 per cent, while spending on outpatients rose 10 per cent.[2] Over the ten-year period from 1972 to 1983, day patients increased by over half a million; from 5 per cent of all inpatients to 17 per cent.[3] Many of these people have come to depend on the community services for the care and attention they might once have received in hospital.

On top of this the closure of the long-stay hospitals and the new emphasis on supporting dependent and semi-dependent people at home, means the community services are being expected to spread their net wider and to cater for a new catchment area. As Enfield and Haringey family practitioner committee recorded in a discussion paper entitled *Primary Care under Pressure*, 'Many of these changes point in the same direction; towards greater pressures on informal care and to greater need for primary care . . . Many of these trends are to be welcomed so long as they are backed up by an adequate development of primary care. The full consequences for primary care of policy changes in the hospital service, have yet to be faced.'[4] One thing we know for sure, however, is that the key to a comprehensive health service now rests with the development of the community services.

The scale and speed of this reorganisation of NHS priorities would have been unthinkable ten years ago; the NHS, like a vast ocean liner, simply did not change course that fast. The new manoeuvrability has been made possible by the enormous increase in the influence of the service's managers and, through them, national policy makers. A tightly managed service with clear vertical lines of authority upwards has dramatically increased the ability of central government, the DHSS and regional health authorities, to steer and shape the course of developments in a way never possible in the past. Rudolf Klein and his colleagues have argued that the new centralisation offers the possibility of bringing about, 'the most important transformation in the history of the NHS'.[5] Since 1948, they maintain, 'the services delivered have reflected as much the idiosyncratic and divergent priorities of local clinicians and health authorities as explicit government policies'. This could now change. We have the prospect, they argue, of an NHS 'that actually lives up to its name — that is a *national* service whose local patterns of provision and activity reflect *national* policies, not only about inputs, but also about outputs'.

It is a measure of the size of the shift since *Patients First* that as recently as 1981, the DHSS was telling health authorities, 'you have a wider opportunity than your predecessors to plan and develop services in the light of *local* needs and circumstances.'[6] Today that is unthinkable.

But what national policies are likely to be reflected by this new centralisation? It has arisen, to a very large extent, out of a period of economic stringency when the need is to make ends meet at a time of falling resources and rising demand. This does not mean that all change can be put down to economic imperatives and the need to increase productivity. The rationalisation of hospitals, both long and short stay, is not just about money; it has roots in changes in our thinking about how to treat dependent people, how to make the best use of scarce and expensive medical resources and even increases in medical understanding which have turned major operations into minor surgery. There is a genuine, progressive and humanitarian conviction that dependent people would usually rather be looked after at home, or in something approximating to it, and that many of us would prefer to be treated as outpatients or day patients. But such good intentions have been severely compromised by the need to save money and savings, which incidentally flow from them, have been used to legitimate falling budgets. Many observers now fear that the switch in NHS priorities is being conducted against a backdrop of dangerously low resources. Figures for NHS funding need to be looked at carefully. As the table shows (see p. 192) real growth in NHS resources, after allowing for inflation, has been small but discernible. Most of this growth, however, has been in the family practitioner service budget, while budgets controlled by health authorities have virtually stood still.

At first sight this might seem encouraging. The family practitioner service is at the heart of community health care and its relative growth appears to reflect the greater importance of the latter. But there is a catch. General practitioners, and the services they provide, are notorious for being unplanned and unevenly distributed across the country and these two factors together have traditionally made them an unreliable vehicle for creating a comprehensive medical service which is co-ordinated and tied in with other areas of NHS activity.

The Conservative government's discussion paper on the future of primary health care, published in the second half of 1986–7, recognises that GP services could be improved, but confines itself to tinkering with the system.[7] It suggests ways in which GPs might be encouraged to provide a more comprehensive and outward-looking service, but shies away from any major administrative changes which would threaten their independence by bringing them more closely under the

RESOURCES AVAILABLE FOR SERVICES 1980/1 TO 1985/6

	1980/1	1981/2	1982/3	1983/4	1984/5	1985/6
Health authority *current spending*						
Total (£m)	6,963	7,681	8,244	8,667	9,161	9,678
Change after inflation (%)		2.0	0.8	0.0	–0.1	0.4
Family practitioner *service* *(current)*						
Total (£m)	2,173	2,504	2,894	3,110	3,419	3,649
Change after inflation (%)		2.0	3.6	2.0	2.8	0.2
NHS total	9,971	11,183	12,197	12,921	13,874	14,724
Change after inflation (%)		2.9	1.5	0.9	1.4	0.6

Source: Social Services Select Committee 1985/6. Public Expenditure on the social services.

umbrella of the rest of the Health Service. They are therefore likely to remain largely unaccountable and un-responsive to the rationalisation of the rest of the NHS.

On top of this, even the most caring GP is not primarily concerned with looking after people who might previously have been looked after in an institution. Much of the new pressure on the community services will come from people who merely need someone to care for them: to change a dressing or administer medication; to help them get out of bed in the morning or go to bed at night; to help them wash or do the shopping. Some GPs may be willing to provide support, though the evidence suggests that many are not, but the backbone of this caring function is provided by district nurses employed by health authorities, care workers employed by social service departments or networks of friends and relatives.

From the NHS's point of view this area of the service is still small, about 10 per cent of all health authority expenditure, and although it has been a priority area for new resources for some years, its growth has been slow. The health authority budget has been more or less static, any significant new growth has had to come out of existing services and, as a consequence, in the last five years or so, the community budget has only grown by about 1 per cent of total NHS expenditure, too small an increase to allow it to keep pace with the increase in demand being placed on it.

A report jointly commissioned by the British Medical Association, the Royal College of Nursing and the Institute of Health Services Management in 1986, argues that funds for both hospital and community services are under 'intense pressure', so intense that 'resources have generally been below that required, even allowing for efficiency savings'.[8]

In a rare, though veiled, attack on government economic policy, Haringey health authority agreed. There is a 'con-siderable body of increasing evidence,' it has written, 'which indicates that the NHS should be funded at a higher level (probably by some 15 per cent), on the basis of present demand and the increasing prominence of the elderly population.'[9]

The results of this under-funding, however, are unlikely to be evenly spread across the country. The infrastructure of the primary health care service, provided by GPs, tends, from the evidence we have accumulated, to work less well in working-class areas. The logical response would be for health authorities to pump in community resources from their own budgets to make up the difference, but, as we have seen, their budgets are too tight to be able to foster policies of positive discrimination in areas of greatest need. As a consequence, the future development of the NHS is likely to reinforce, rather than diminish, existing patterns of inequality in access to health care, and redistributive mechanisms like RAWP are unlikely to do much to diminish this.

The RAWP formula has not only been overtaken by cutbacks in NHS funding, it expressly excludes any measures of the adequacy of family practitioner services. It is therefore largely irrelevant to the development of community health care, even though this is the only significant area of growth in the NHS in the foreseeable future and, to this extent, represents *the* future of public health provision. Moreover, even in RAWP-losing areas like Haringey, the better off, the better informed and the more mobile sections of the population are in a position to minimise the impact of the relative cut-back by playing the system — travelling elsewhere or demanding attention. The real losers are people who cannot afford to buy their way out of the public sector, may not know what they are entitled to and even if they do, are not in a strong position to get it.

Nor is the development of comprehensive community services likely to be helped by the new managerial thrust in Health Service administration which has switched attention from inputs to outputs, or, put another way, from resources going into the NHS and the needs that are clamouring to be met, to how the NHS can maximise its productivity and increase throughputs. Thus, in a period of economic stringency, management becomes an exercise in trying to squeeze a quart out of a pint pot, rather than challenging the broad parameters within which it is being expected to operate. Such thinking may well undermine a comprehensive community service. It is likely to provide a powerful incentive to health authorities to fall back on the management techniques which have enabled them to make such dramatic increases in efficiency in the hospital service. The trouble is that these techniques have difficulty recognising the nature of caring for people. Caring is not about what you do but how you do it. It is about attitudes and feelings; the difference between getting an elderly person up in the morning and helping *them* to get up; between dressing them and helping them to dress; between treating patients and helping them to look after themselves. Caring is difficult for an activity, or performance-based management system to evaluate and the risk is that in looking for greater productivity or throughput, the new management will lose sight of the qualitative aspects of the caring relationship.

There is, arguably, a counterveiling tendency to this. The emphasis on outputs has also stimulated a new awareness of issues of quality, an area the NHS has never been good at in the past beyond the basic issues of whether or not a patient lives or dies. The Griffiths team, drawing to some degree on its commercial background, argued that this was not good enough. As we have already noted, the report stated: 'Businessmen have a keen sense of how well they are looking after their customers. Whether the NHS is meeting the needs of its patients and the community, and can prove that it is doing so, is open to question.'

It is indeed. At one level most people are profoundly grateful for the care and attention they receive from a doctor or nurse but at another there are a myriad of small complaints which add up to quite a substantial measure of dissatisfaction with the Health Service. Among the commonest are complaints about poor information, lack of individual attention, disregard for an individual's feelings and opinions or just plain bad hospital food.

These complaints may mean no more than a need for a mechanism which allows people to express their views and to feel confident that they will affect events. There is a feel about the Health Service of a monolithic and impersonal enterprise which does not care whether you are happy or not and it is doubly difficult to complain because most people are aware that it is under enormous pressures; guilt about complaining comes easily. There needs to be a mechanism for collecting and monitoring consumer opinion and feeding this into the works. The collection system need be no more sophisticated than the sort of basic, standard, questionnaire every hotel leaves lying about in its rooms. Some health authorities have begun to do this.

They have also begun to look at ways of fostering greater awareness among staff on issues of quality. Some health authorities are experimenting with quality control circles, many have appointed quality control managers for the first time and some are running courses in what is known as 'shop window dressing', an expression taken from the commercial sector. Haringey is one of them. 'There is some evidence that customer/professional relationships are not always being handled with sufficient professionalism and there may be room for improvement in this area,' a training document from the authority explained.

It is at this point that the whole exercise becomes a little suspect. Good consumer relations is not a solution to poor funding and inadequate staffing and in many situations, staff are already only too aware that what they are providing is less adequate than it should be and perhaps less adequate than it used to be. Rightly or wrongly they feel they are being forced, by circumstances outside their control, to accept lower standards. For quality to mean anything they have got to be able to believe that it is within their control to provide a good service in the first place so that any falling off from it is clearly their responsibility and something they can alter. Without this, how much substance is there likely to be behind the toothpaste, airline hostess, smiles that receptionists, nurses and perhaps even doctors may be expected to wear in the future?

It is hard to escape the conclusion that the main forces shaping the NHS today – money and managerialism – appear to be pushing it away from its original aspirations of equality and comprehensiveness, increasing the search for individual and private solutions, and thereby reducing the quality of life of those who cannot afford to do this. People like Stan Field will be the first to suffer.

Notes

Chapter 1

1. *'Guide to hospital waiting lists 1985'*, *Inter-authority comparisons and consultancy*, The College of Health, November 1985.
2. 'Operation waiting list "gets longer" ', *Guardian*, London, 8 December 1985.
3. *Unsafe in their Hands*, Report from the Radical Statistics Health Group, London, April 1985.
4. Jeanette Mitchell, *What is to be Done About Illness and Health?*, Penguin, London, 1984.
5. Personal communication.
6. James Dean, *The Urban Growth of Haringey*, local history department, Haringey Public Libraries.
7. *Ibid.*
8. Statistics for socio-economic well-being in Haringey can be found in the strategic and operational plans, published by Haringey Health District. Haringey community health council has also produced a district population profile.
9. *A Happier Old Age*, HMSO, 1978.
10. *Mental Handicap. Progress, Problems and Priorities*, DHSS, 1980. More general figures also available in *Priorities for the Health and Personal Social Services in England*, HMSO, 1976.
11. P. Townsend and N. Davidson (Eds.), *Inequalities in Health, The Black Report*, Penguin, London, 1980.
12. Draft district operational plan, 1987/88–1989/90, Haringey Health District.
13. Draft strategic plan, 1983/93, Haringey Health District.

Chapter 2

1. David Owen, *In Sickness and in Health*, Quartet, London, 1976.

2. *Sharing Resources for Health in England*, report of the Resources Allocation Working Party, HMSO, 1976.
3. *Priorities in the Health and Personal Social Services in England, op. cit.*
4. Judy Allsop, *Health Policy and the National Health Service*, Longman, London, 1984.
5. See reports of the committees of inquiry into Ely Hospital, HMSO, 1969, Whittenham Hospital, HMSO, 1972, South Ockendon Hospital, HMSO, 1974, and Normansfield Hospital, HMSO, 1978.
6. Quoted in Allsop, *op. cit.*, p. 109.
7. *The Way Forward. Priorities in the Health and Social Services*, DHSS, 1977.
8. Taken from DHSS figures.
9. *Chronic and Critical. The long crisis in London's everyday health care*, a discussion document commissioned by Community Health Councils in London, September, 1980.
10. Annual report, Haringey Community Health Council, 1979/80.
11. Draft strategic plan 1983/93, Haringey Health District.
12. *Patients First*, consultative paper on the structure and management of the NHS, DHSS, 1979.
13. *The National Health Service Management Inquiry (Griffiths) Report*, DHSS, 1983.
14. 'Up-dating the performance package', *Health and Social Service Journal*, 20 June 1985.
15. Rudolf Klein, 'Auditing the National Health Service', *British Medical Journal*, Vol. 285, p. 672.
16. Report of working party on performance indicators, DHSS, 1985.
17. *The Health Services*, November 1983.
18. *Value for money developments in the National Health Service*, National Audit Office, HMSO, February 1986.
19. *Ibid.*
20. Alan Maynard and Nick Bosanquet, *Public expenditure on the NHS, Recent trends and future problems*, Institute of Health Service Management, September 1986.
21. *National Health Service Economic Review*, 1986, National Association of Health Authorities.
22. Rudolf Klein et al, *British Medical Journal*, Vol. 290, 1 June 1985.
23. Maynard and Bosanquet, *op. cit.*

Chapter 3

1. Research project conducted by the National Association of Health Authorities, October 1986.

2. *Medical Education*, 4th report from the Social Services Select Committee, session 1980/81, HMSO, 1981.
3. 'Longer wait for surgery "causing crisis in NHS" ', *Guardian*, London, 20 June 1986.
4. 'Acute wards "squeezed" to meet bill for elderly', *Guardian*, London, 24 June 1986.
5. Richard Taylor, *Medicine Out of Control. The Anatomy of a Malignant Technology*, Sun Books, Melbourne, 1979.
6. *Ibid.*
7. *National Health Service control of nursing manpower*, National Audit Office, HMSO, July 1985.
8. Len Peach, chairman of the NHS Management Board, circular to regional general managers, 13 June 1986.
9. *'Nursing crisis hits hospitals'*, *Guardian*, London, 27 November 1987.
10. Survey of nursing stress, *Nursing Mirror*, 26 June 1985.
11. Reported in *Health and Social Service Journal*, 19 September 1985, on study by Peter Hingley at Bristol Polytechnic.
12. *The Economist*, London, 3 March 1984.
13. Alison Dunn, 'Care on Contract', *Lampada*, No. 5, pp. 8–12, Autumn 1985.
14. *Guide to hospital waiting lists, 1985, Inter-authority comparisons and consultancy*, *op. cit.*
15. Survey commissioned by the British Medical Association, February 1985.
16. 'Waiting on the Threshold of Pain', the *Independent*, London, 14 October 1986.

Chapter 4

1. *Royal Commission on the National Health Service*, HMSO, Cmnd 7615, July 1979.
2. See, for instance, the *Royal Commission on the National Health Service*, (*Ibid*), *Primary health care in inner London*, the London Health Planning Consortium, 1981, and B. Jarman, *Survey of Primary Health Care in London*, occasional paper 16, Royal College of General Practice, 1981.
3. Townsend and Davidson, *op. cit.*
4. J. Tudor Hart, 'The Inverse Care Law', *Lancet*, Vol. 1, 1971.
5. Study of Manchester GPs, quoted in 'Family doctors' rest cures', *Guardian*, London, 1 December 1984.
6. Rudolf Klein, *The Politics of the National Health Service*, p. 97, Longman, London, 1983.
7. *Ibid*, p. 138.

8. Quoted in R. G. S. Brown, *The Changing National Health Service*, p. 83, Routledge & Kegan Paul, London, 1978.
9. *Royal Commission on the National Health Service*, *op. cit.*
10. Personal correspondence, figures issued by Haringey Health District.
11. *Primary Health Care, An Agenda for Discussion*, HMSO, April 1986.
12. District Operational Plan, 1985/86–1987/88, Haringey Health District.

Chapter 5

1. See note 5, Chapter 2.
2. See the House of Commons social services select committee report, 1984/85, *Community care with special reference to adult mentally ill and mentally handicapped people*, HMSO, 1985.
3. Allsop, *op. cit.*
4. Wolfenden Committee, *The Future of Voluntary Organisations*, Croom Helm, 1977.
5. Allsop, *op. cit.*
6. House of Commons social services select committee, *op. cit.*
7. Maynard and Bosanquet, *op. cit.*
8. House of Commons social services select committee, *op. cit.*
9. Letter to *The Sunday Times*, 7 August 1983; Marjorie Wallace's article appeared under the headline 'Bedsit Despair of the Mental Hospital Outcasts', *The Sunday Times*, London, 20 November 1983.
10. *Mental Health and the Community*, Richmond Fellowship, 1983.
11. Dr Malcolm Weller, 'Crime and Psychopathology', *British Medical Journal* correspondence, 4 January 1986.
12. House of Commons social services committee, *op. cit.*
13. Weller, *op. cit.*
14. House of Commons social services select committee, *op. cit.*
15. Daphne Cloag, 'Community Care. Rhetoric and Action', *British Medical Journal*, 16 November 1986.
16. *Care in Action: Handbook of Policies and Priorities for the Health and Personal Social Services in England*, HMSO, 1981.
17. *Care in the Community. A Consultative Document on Moving Resources for Care in England*, DHSS, 1981.
18. *Even Better Services? A Critical Review of Mental Health Policies in the 1970s*, Campaign for the Mentally Handicapped, 1982.
19. 'The Shameful Secrets', *Guardian*, London, 20 July 1983.
20. House of Commons social services select committee, *op. cit.*

Chapter 6

1. *National Health Service Economic Review*, National Association of Health Authorities, 1986.

2. Annual report, Enfield and Haringey family practitioner committee, 1986.
3. *Public Expenditure on the National Health Service. Recent trends and the outlook*, Institute of Health Service Management, 1985.
4. Discussion paper issued by the Enfield and Haringey family practitioner committee, March 1986.
5. R. Klein et al, *British Medical Journal*, Vol. 290, 1 June 1985.
6. *Ibid.*
7. *Primary Health Care: An Agenda for Discussion*, HMSO, April 1986.
8. Maynard and Bosanquet, *op. cit.*
9. Draft strategic plan 1983/93, Haringey Health District.

Index

189–90; district general, 71–8, 87; 'dowry' system, 181–3; geriatric, 34, 175; in Haringey, 18, 19–20, 33–40, 57, 59, 60–111; junior medical staff, 35–7, 64; manpower cuts, 52–4; out-patients, 63, 69, 86, 109, 121, 189; performance indicators 48–9; planning population of, 57–8, 73; psychiatric (long-stay), 59, 156, 157–62, 168–73, 181–2, 183–4, 188, 190; rationalisation/closure of, 31–2, 33–40, 59, 142, 147, 155, 181–2, 183–4, 190, 191; reduced length of stay in, 49, 154, 175–6; rehabilitation of patients, 169–73; 'revolving door syndrome', 154–5, 175; teaching, 35–6, 80, 91, 147; waiting lists, 2–3, 64, 108–10; *see also* North Middlesex hospital

'hotel services', hospital, 64, 65, 93–4, 96–106

House of Commons National Audit Office study on nursing (1985), 64, 89, 90

House of Commons Public Accounts Committee, 42, 50–1, 52

House of Commons Social Services Select Committee, 82, 165, 168–9, 187–8

ill health, causes of, 4–5

infant mortality ratio, 16

infectious diseases, 75

institutional care, institutionalisation, *v.* community care, 28–31, 155–74, 175–6, 186; *see also* hospitals

Inverse Care Law, 122–3, 151

Isenburg, Dr Harry, 115–16, 121

'items of service' payment, GP's, 136–7

Jenkin, Patrick, 164–5

junior hospital staff, 35–7, 64, 81–4, 87; *see also* nurses

Karmali, Dr Nurjahan, 112–15, 119, 121

Klein, Rudolf, 48, 126, 127, 131, 190–1

laboratory technicians, 53

Labour government, 23, 24; Priorities document, 27–31, 32–3, 155, 163; RAWP formula, 25–7, 32, 33; *The Way Forward*, 31–2

laundry service, hospital, 93, 94; contracting out of, 96, 98, 101

League of Friends, 158–9

local councils, 17–18

local government reorganisation (1965), 10, 14

London ambulance service, 186, 189

long-stay services *see* caring services

managerialism, new, 22–59, 152, 190–1, 194–5, 197; cost cutting, 49–51; cost improvement programme, 51–2, 54, 56; in Haringey, 56–9; manpower, 52–4; performance, 46–9

Marsh, George, 73, 74, 78, 79, 83

maternity hospitals, 34

meals on wheels, 29, 180

medical inflation, 27

medical practices committee, 134

medical technologies, increasing costs of, 72, 73

mentally ill and handicapped people, 16, 20, 80, 81, 84, 150; children, 175; community/caring services for, 28, 29–30, 146, 155, 157, 162–74, 175–8, 179, 181–4; elderly, 176–8; institutional care for, 157–62, 166, 167, 168–73, 175–6, 181–2, 183–4, 188

Middlesex executive committee, 128

'mixed economy of welfare' concept, 164–5, 182

Morris, Liz, 177, 179